HUMAN AGGRESSION

Born in 1920, Anthony Storr was educated at Winchester, Christ's College, Cambridge, and Westminster Hospital. After qualifying as a doctor in 1944, he specialized in psychiatry and held posts at Runwell Mental Hospital and at the Maudsley Hospital. He also trained as an analyst in the school of C. C. Jung, though he prefers not to be labelled as an adherent of any one analytical school. His publications include *The Integrity of the Personality* (1960), *Sexual Deviation* (1964), *Human Aggression* (1968), *Human Destructiveness* (1972), *The Dynamics of Creation* (1972), *The Art of Psychotherapy* (1979), *Solitude* (1988), *Freud* (1989) and *Churchill's Black Dog and Other Phenomena of the Human Mind* (1989). He has also edited *Jung Selected Writings* (1983). He has contributed reviews and articles to many papers, including the *Sunday Times*, *The Times Literary Supplement* and the *Spectator*. Dr Storr was Clinical Lecturer in Psychiatry, University of Oxford, from 1974 to 1984. He was Fellow of Green College, Oxford, from 1979 to 1984 and is now Emeritus Professor.

HUMAN AGGRESSION

Anthony Storr

Penguin Books

PENGUIN BOOKS

Published by the Penguin Group
Penguin Books Ltd, 27 Wrights Lane, London W8 5TZ, England
Penguin Books USA Inc., 375 Hudson Street, New York, New York 10014, USA
Penguin Books Australia Ltd, Ringwood, Victoria, Australia
Penguin Books Canada Ltd, 10 Alcorn Avenue, Toronto, Ontario, Canada M4V 3B2
Penguin Books (NZ) Ltd, 182–190 Wairau Road, Auckland 10, New Zealand

Penguin Books Ltd, Registered Offices: Harmondsworth, Middlesex, England

First published by Allen Lane The Penguin Press 1968
Published in Pelican Books 1970
Reprinted in Penguin Books 1992
10 9 8 7 6 5 4 3 2 1

Printed in England by Clays Ltd, St Ives plc
Set in Linotype Times

To Konrad Lorenz
with admiration and affection

Contents

Introduction   9

1. Psycho-Analysis and the 'Death Instinct'   15

2. Is Aggression an Instinct?   27

3. Aggression in Social Structure   39

4. Territory and Ritual   51

5. Aggression in Childhood Development   60

6. Aggression in Adult Life   74

7. Aggression in the Relation Between the Sexes   85

8. Aggression in Relation to Depression   101

9. Schizoid Defences against Hostility   114

10. Paranoid Hostility   124

11. Psychopathic Hostility   137

12. Ways of Reducing Hostility   147

Further Reading   166

Index   167

7

Introduction

That man is an aggressive creature will hardly be disputed. With the exception of certain rodents, no other vertebrate habitually destroys members of his own species. No other animal takes positive pleasure in the exercise of cruelty upon another of his own kind. We generally describe the most repulsive examples of man's cruelty as brutal or bestial, implying by these adjectives that such behaviour is characteristic of less highly developed animals than ourselves. In truth, however, the extremes of 'brutal' behaviour are confined to man; and there is no parallel in nature to our savage treatment of each other. The sombre fact is that we are the cruellest and most ruthless species that has ever walked the earth; and that, although we may recoil in horror when we read in newspaper or history book of the atrocities committed by man upon man, we know in our hearts that each one of us harbours within himself those same savage impulses which lead to murder, to torture and to war.

To write about human aggression is a difficult task because the term is used in so many different senses. Aggression is one of those words which everyone knows, but which is nevertheless hard to define. As psychologists and psychiatrists use it, it covers a very wide range of human behaviour. The red-faced infant squalling for the bottle is being aggressive; and so is the judge who awards a thirty-year sentence for robbery. The guard in a concentration camp who tortures his helpless victim is obviously acting aggressively. Less manifestly, but no less certainly, so is the neglected wife who threatens or attempts suicide in order to regain her husband's affection. When a word becomes so diffusely applied that it is used both of the competitive striving of a footballer and also of the bloody violence of a murderer, it ought either to be dropped or else more closely defined. Aggression is a portmanteau term which is fairly bursting at its seams. Yet, until we can more clearly designate and comprehend the various aspects of human behaviour which are subsumed under this head, we cannot discard the concept.

One difficulty is that there is no clear dividing line between those forms of aggression which we all deplore and those which we must not disown if we are to survive. When a child rebels against authority it is being aggressive: but it is also manifesting a drive towards independence which is a necessary and valuable part of growing up. The desire for power has, in extreme form, disastrous aspects which we all acknowledge: but the drive to conquer difficulties, or to gain mastery over the external world, underlies the greatest of human achievements. Some writers define aggression as 'that response which follows frustration', or as 'an act whose goal-response is injury to an organism (or organism surrogate)'.[1] In the author's view these definitions impose limits upon the concept of aggression which are not in accord with the underlying facts of human nature which the word is attempting to express. It is worth noticing, for instance, that the words we use to describe intellectual effort are aggressive words. We *attack* problems, or *get our teeth into* them. We *master* a subject when we have

10

struggled with and *overcome* its difficulties. We *sharpen* our wits, hoping that our mind will develop *a keen edge* in order that we may better *dissect* a problem into its component parts. Although intellectual tasks are often frustrating, to argue that all intellectual effort is the result of frustration is to impose too negative a colouring upon the positive impulse to comprehend and master the external world.

The aggressive part of human nature is not only a necessary safeguard against predatory attack. It is also the basis of intellectual achievement, of the attainment of independence, and even of that proper pride which enables a man to hold his head high amongst his fellows. This is no new conception. The historian Gibbon, in a famous passage, displays a very similar idea of human nature to that which psychotherapists profess. Whereas the latter refer to sexual instincts and aggressive instincts, Gibbon writes of 'the love of pleasure and the love of action':

There are two very natural propensities which we may distinguish in the most virtuous and liberal dispositions, the love of pleasure and the love of action. If the former be refined by art and learning, improved by the charms of social intercourse, and corrected by a just regard to economy, to health, and to reputation, it is productive of the greatest part of the happiness of private life. The love of action is a principle of a much stronger and more doubtful nature. It often leads to anger, to ambition, and to revenge; but, when it is guided by the sense of propriety and benevolence, it becomes the parent of every virtue; and, if those virtues are accompanied with equal abilities, a family, a state, or an empire may be indebted for their safety and prosperity to the undaunted courage of a single man. To the love of pleasure we may therefore ascribe most of the agreeable, to the love of action we may attribute most of the useful and respectable qualifications. The character in which both the one and the other should be united and harmonized would seem to constitute the most perfect idea of

11

human nature. The insensible and inactive disposition, which should be supposed alike destitute of both, would be rejected, by the common consent of mankind, as utterly incapable of procuring any happiness to the individual or any public benefit to the world. But it was not in *this* world that the primitive Christians were desirous of making themselves either agreeable or useful.[2]

Gibbon recognizes quite clearly that the most deplorable manifestations of aggression share identical roots with valuable and essential parts of human endeavour. Without the aggressive, active side of his nature man would be even less able than he is to direct the course of his life or to influence the world around him. In fact, it is obvious that man could never have attained his present dominance, nor even have survived as a species, unless he possessed a large endowment of aggressiveness.

It is a tragic paradox that the very qualities which have led to man's extraordinary success are also those most likely to destroy him. His ruthless drive to subdue or to destroy every apparent obstacle in his path does not stop short at his own fellows; and since he now possesses weapons of unparalleled destructiveness and also apparently lacks the built-in safeguards which prevent most animals from killing others of the same species, it is not beyond possibility that he may yet encompass the total elimination of *homo sapiens*.

What follows are the reflections of a psychotherapist upon the aggressive component in human nature. The views which are put forward are anything but dogmatic. All psychotherapists suffer from the fact that, although their knowledge of a few people may be rather profound, their conclusions are necessarily drawn from a limited and highly selected sample of the population. Moreover, many of the theories which are available in the practice of psychotherapy are difficult to substantiate scientifically, because the psychotherapist is endeavouring to deal with the person as a whole. Psychologists working in laboratories can construct experiments in which, for example, aggressive emotions can be more or less separately aroused and studied; and the conclusions which they reach can be statistically expressed. The disadvantage of nearly all such experiments is that the situations upon which they are based are so restricted that they are far removed from life as it is lived. Aggression, for example, is inextricably mingled with fear and sex in many situations. It is very much to be hoped that, in time, there will be a *rapprochement* between the precise but limited viewpoint of the experimentalist, and the less defined but wider conceptions of the psychotherapist. In the meantime, we must do the best we can with incomplete and unproved hypotheses.

The present preoccupation of Western society with the problem of aggression is, of course, dictated by the fear of destruction by nuclear weapons which overhangs us all. The problem of war is more compelling than ever before in history. The complexities of the circumstances which provoke war are such that no one man and no one viewpoint can possibly comprehend them all. Anyone who promises a solution to a problem so perennial is too arrogant to be trusted; and no such solution will be put forward here. The author believes, however, that if stability in world affairs is ever to be achieved, the psychological point of view deserves equal consideration with the political, economic and other aspects. The study of human aggression and its control is, therefore, relevant to the problem of war although, alone, it cannot possibly provide a complete answer.

References

1. Dollard, J., *et al.*, *Frustration and Aggression* (London: Routledge & Kegan Paul, 1944), p. 8.
2. Gibbon, Edward, *The History of the Decline and Fall of the Roman Empire* (London: Methuen, 1897), vol. II, pp. 34–5.

One

Psycho-Analysis and the 'Death Instinct'

Since aggressive behaviour is so characteristic of man, it might be supposed that the origin and determinants of human aggression would, long ago, have been established and agreed. Such, however, is not the case; and there is still considerable dispute as to whether aggression is an inborn, instinctive drive which, like the sexual instinct, seeks spontaneous expression, or whether, on the contrary, it is merely a response to adverse external circumstances and not instinctive at all. In this chapter, some aspects of Freud's view of aggression will be discussed and criticized. Although I believe that in some respects his views were mistaken, his influence has been so powerful, and his enrichment of our understanding of ourselves so enormous, that, although his idea of a 'death instinct' is no longer accepted, it cannot possibly be disregarded.

During the past sixty years, psycho-analysts and psycho-therapists of every school have become increasingly preoccupied with aggression; but it cannot be said that the results of their inquiries and speculations are entirely happy, in spite of the great importance of their contribution to our thinking on the subject. Some have accepted the idea that man is not naturally aggressive, but only becomes so as the result of frustration. Others have postulated an innate aggressive impulse, but have supposed that this is in origin destructively directed against the self, and only becomes turned outwards against other people or the world in general as a secondary phenomenon. It is widely accepted that the infant is potentially aggressive from the moment of birth, and psycho-analysts with special experience in treating small children claim that even infants inevitably entertain destructive phantasies of terrifying intensity.

These phantasies, it is admitted, arise partly from innate aggressiveness. Even psycho-analysts recognize that there are inborn temperamental differences between babies, so that one may be more placid, more greedy, or more active than another. However, the principal concern of psycho-analysis is with nurture rather than with nature; so that it is not surprising that analysts attribute even more importance to a hostile or unfavourable environment as the source of infantile aggression than they do to innate factors. Environmental frustration is, of course, inevitable, for no human baby can be granted, although he may expect, a mother who fulfils his every need without delay. Psycho-analysts are well aware of this; but since they are engaged in discovering in what ways their patients' earliest needs have not been met, and since the consequence of parental failure to fulfil infantile requirements is generally frustrated rage, psycho-analysts are apt to take too negative a view of aggression, and to neglect the more positive aspects to which, in the introduction to this book, attention was directed. In general, there is a tendency amongst psycho-analysts to treat aggression as pathological; and to suppose that, although there may be some inborn disposition towards aggressiveness, men ought to be able to rid themselves of it by securing a perfect environment for their children, or, failing this, by later subjecting them to psycho-analysis.

The following quotation from a paper of Melanie Klein's aptly illustrates this point:

> One cannot help wondering whether psycho-analysis is not destined to go beyond the single individual in its range of operation and influence the life of mankind as a whole. ... It cannot it is true altogether do away with man's aggressive instinct as such; but it can, by diminishing the anxiety which accentuates those instincts, break up the mutual reinforcement that is going on all the time between his hatred and his fear.... We are ready to believe that what would now seem a Utopian state of things may well come true in those distant days when, as I hope, child-analysis will become as much a part of every person's upbringing as school education is now. Then perhaps, that hostile attitude, springing from fear and suspicion, which is latent more or less strongly in each human being, and which intensifies a hundredfold in him every impulse of destruction, will give way to kindlier and more trustful feelings towards his fellow-men, and people may inhabit the world together in greater peace and good-will than they do now.[1]

Mrs Klein's Utopian vision is a product of her therapeutic enthusiasm and hopefulness for no one was more aware than she of how aggressive human beings can be.

Indeed, the analytical situation is one in which the emergence of aggressive emotion is not only tolerated but encouraged; and it might be justly alleged that analysts are far more keenly conscious than most people of the murderous impulses which can be discerned within us all. Nevertheless, the historical development of psycho-analytic thought has been such that, although man's aggressiveness has at last been fully recognized, most writers have given the impression that it is merely a deplorable impulse which ought to be eliminated rather than a necessary part of our biological inheritance with which we have to learn to co-exist, and which has served and serves to preserve us.

Human Aggression

When Freud began his researches into the human mind towards the close of the nineteenth century, he paid little attention to aggression. Neither the word 'aggression' nor the word 'sadism' occurs in the index to *The Interpretation of Dreams*, which was first published in 1900; and in *Three Essays on the Theory of Sexuality*, published in 1905, aggression is regarded as a part-component of the sexual instinct:

The sexuality of most male human beings contains an element of aggressiveness – a desire to subjugate; the biological significance of it seems to lie in the need for overcoming the resistance of the sexual object by means other than the process of wooing. Thus sadism would correspond to an aggressive component of the sexual instinct which has become independent and exaggerated, and, by displacement, has usurped the leading position.[2]

At this early date, it is natural that Freud should have allotted so little importance to aggression compared with sexuality. In nineteenth-century Vienna, the mental climate was one in which sex was a secret, and hence a problem; a subject which could not be freely discussed, and around which hung a cloud of guilt and dubiety. It is entirely understandable that, in this atmosphere, sex should have appeared to be the only mainspring of human conflict. It is also probable that Freud, like other creative geniuses, fell in love with his own ideas, with the result that he was initially reluctant to modify them. It required considerable courage to advance his theories of infantile sexuality, against a current of almost universal obloquy; and the opposition which he encountered may well have confirmed him in his inclination to attribute neurotic disturbances exclusively to disorders of sexual development, and to regard sex as the only prime mover of human conduct.

Moreover, many of Freud's early patients seem to have

been cases of hysteria – or what is now called anxiety-hysteria. It is such patients, especially, who suffer from long-standing repression of sexuality, and who therefore conceal both from themselves and from others the sexual aspects of their nature. It is also to such cases that psycho-analysis in its pristine form can be applied with the greatest practical and theoretical success.

Freud himself admitted his reluctance to acknowledge the existence of aggression as a separate entity.

I can remember my own defensive attitude when the idea of an instinct of destruction first made its appearance in psycho-analytical literature, and how long it took before I became accessible to it.[3]

There can be little doubt that this defensive attitude had been reinforced by the fact that, quite early in the history of the psycho-analytic movement, one of its principal members had come to the conclusion that the aggressive component in human nature was more important than sexuality. Alfred Adler, whose contribution to our understanding of man is often under-estimated, believed that 'striving for superiority' was the dominant motive of human beings; and it was because of his insistence upon this that, in 1911, he finally parted company with Freud and psycho-analysis. Adler's concept became progressively modified during his lifetime, to judge from the changing phrases in which he expressed it. According to Ernest Jones, it was as early as 1908 that Adler suggested that there might be a primary aggressive instinct. This was later expressed as a 'will to power'; which, in its turn, was superseded by the phrase 'striving for superiority'. In his final writings, Adler referred to this same instinct as the 'striving for perfection', or 'upward striving'; a concept so abstract and metaphysical that it cannot be distinguished from Bergson's *élan vital* or

19

Shaw's life-force. That this was not how his original idea appeared to others at the time of his split with Freud is attested by the latter's caustic comment on some lectures which Adler was to give in America. 'Presumably the object is to save the world from sexuality and base it on aggression.'[4] To have acknowledged the idea of a primary aggressive instinct directed towards the external world would have meant that psycho-analysis moved closer towards the acceptance of Adler's 'striving for superiority'. At this time this would have been impossible for Freud, who was fully engaged in trying to get his theory of sexuality established, and who was therefore intolerant of any divergence from his conceptions, as we are all inclined to be when tending the growth of those delicate plants, our new ideas. Whether or not Adler's defection contributed to Freud's reluctance to recognize aggression, it was not until 1915, when Freud was already fifty-nine, that he first wrote of aggression as primary and distinct from sexuality. By 1920, this new conception had been elaborated into the theory of the 'death instinct' which made its appearance in *Beyond the Pleasure Principle*. This theory is one of the stranger by-ways of thought, and the majority of psychologists have never accepted it. Freud, when he at last came to recognize that there was something like an aggressive instinct in man, surprisingly concluded that this was primarily self-destructive rather than directed towards mastering the external world. Man's aggression was a secondary phenomenon, a diversion of the energy of the 'death instinct', away from the self against which it was initially directed. Freud's final view, which he never modified, came to be that there were simply two groups of instincts:

Erotic instincts which are always trying to collect living substances together into even larger unities, and the death instincts, which act against that tendency and try to bring living matter back into an inorganic condition. The cooperation and opposition of these two forces produce the phenomena of life to which death puts an end.[5]

The idea of the death instinct has been criticized on many grounds, not least because the conception of instinct as self-destructive runs counter to the biological view of instinctive patterns as those which tend to preserve life and encourage the reproduction of living organisms. In spite of the title which Freud gave to the book in which he elaborated the concept of the death instinct, his thinking was still dominated by the pleasure principle, which formed the main theoretical prop of all his early work.

In the psycho-analytical theory of the mind we take it for granted that the course of mental processes is automatically regulated by the pleasure principle: that is to say, we believe that any given process originates in an unpleasant state of tension and thereupon determines for itself such a path that its ultimate issue coincides with the relaxation of this tension, i.e. with avoidance of pain or with production of pleasure.[6]

Freud considered that the ideal state at which man was aiming was one of blissful satiation, like that which he supposedly experienced in earliest infancy.

No one who has seen a baby sinking back satisfied from the breast and falling asleep with flushed cheeks and a blissful smile can escape the reflection that this picture persists as a prototype of the experience of sexual satisfaction in later life.[7]

The facts that have led us to believe in the supremacy of the pleasure-principle in psychic life also find expression in the hypothesis that there is an attempt on the part of the psychic apparatus to keep the quantity of excitation present as low as possible, or at least constant. This is the same supposition only put into another form, for, if the psychic apparatus operates in the direction of keeping down the quantity of excitation, all

21

that tends to increase it must be felt to be contrary to function, that is to say, painful.[8]

This picture of the organism ridding itself of tension, and of wishing always for total relaxation into a state of Boeotian bliss, lies at the root of Freud's thinking about instinct, and accounts for his failure to see in aggression anything other than a destructive force. The search for stimulation, for obstacles to be overcome, for achievement, or for power, is alien to a concept of man in which pleasure is attained only by ridding oneself of tension, and sinking back into that state of Nirvana with which Freud believed that all infants began their existence, and from which the trauma of birth was supposed unkindly to arouse them. With this presupposition in mind, it is not surprising that Freud came to believe that every living creature was in a sense instinctively driven towards death; since death is the state in which the organism has totally rid itself of tension, the final regression beyond infancy and conception to that earliest state of all, before life itself made its appearance.

It would be counter to the conservative nature of instinct if the goal of life were a state never hitherto reached. It must rather be an ancient starting point, which the living being left long ago, and to which it harks back again by all the circuitous paths of development. If we may assume an experience admitting of no exception that everything living dies from causes within itself, and returns to the inorganic, we can only say 'The goal of all life is death' and, casting back, 'The inanimate was there before the animate'.[9]

In this view the death instinct is a kind of personification of the second law of thermodynamics: a sombre acknowledgement that dissolution and dispersal is the inevitable fate of all organizations of matter, whether animate or inanimate. But, although we must admit that entropy constantly increases, and that there may be forces within us which lead to our final demise, it is surely unjustifiable to assume that those forces are to be subsumed under the same heading as those instincts which serve to preserve us or encourage us to reproduce.

Freud's concept of the death instinct need not have detained us were it not that it has influenced so many subsequent writers, including some who came to disagree with many of his formulations, of whom the most distinguished is Melanie Klein. In Freud's view, aggression against the external world in general and other people in particular was ultimately the result of the death instinct being blocked by erotic and self-preservative instincts. Although the death instinct must finally conquer, since we all have to die, it was thought that, so long as life persisted, its natural expression was inhibited. Although the acceptance of a death instinct is in one sense an admission of a primary aggressive drive, yet the concept still implies that aggression directed against the external world is a secondary phenomenon which would not exist unless the primary instinct was being blocked or interfered with. Thus, although those who hopefully believe that man's aggression is invariably the result of frustration have not necessarily accepted the existence of a death instinct, yet there is nothing even in Freud's later work which would support the idea of a positive, primary aggressive drive; and hence nothing which is obviously opposed to the idea that some kind of frustration is always antecedent to aggression.

Melanie Klein, Freud's most distinguished successor in the psycho-analytic field, whose hopes for the future have already been noted, laid especial emphasis upon aggression, which she conceived to be operative within the infant from the very beginning of life. It is extremely difficult objectively to test Kleinian concepts; since they depend upon the idea that the infant soon comes to possess an inner world of phantasy in which violent emotions of love and hate alternate and intermingle, but which is inaccessible to direct observation. The existence of this inner world is chiefly surmised from the later recollections of children and adults in analysis. Since memory is notoriously unreliable, and since, moreover, early phantasies pertain to a period of life long before the infant is capable of speech, Mrs Klein's concepts are best regarded as a provisional explanatory scheme which serves to orientate the explorer in the maze of infantile development, but which cannot yet be awarded the dignity of a scientific hypothesis, since it is incapable of proof or disproof by any methods at our disposal. This is not to denigrate Mrs Klein's achievement. Her creative imagination has provided the analyst with a working scheme which makes comprehensible psychological phenomena which must otherwise remain obscure; but it is important to remember that any picture of what takes place in the infant psyche must, unavoidably, be more in the nature of an explanatory myth than a statement of fact, and it is thus even more susceptible of modification than a scientifically testable theory.

Melanie Klein's view is that there is an innate conflict between love and hate in every baby which is present from the moment of birth or may even exist prenatally. She believed that the 'capacity both for love and for destructive impulses is, to some extent, constitutional, though varying individually in strength and interacting from the beginning with external conditions'.[10] So violent is this aggressive drive, that the infant experiences intense anxiety both about the possible destruction of those who care for him and also about the chance of his own destruction:

The struggle between life and death instincts and the ensu-

24

ing threat of annihilation of the self and of the object by destructive impulses are fundamental factors in the infant's initial relation to his mother.[11]

In spite of the fact that Melanie Klein accepted that 'Destructive impulses, varying from individual to individual, are an integral part of mental life, even in favourable circumstances'[12] she still believed that these impulses were derived from a re-direction of the death instinct towards the external world. She also habitually writes of aggression in terms of hate, greed, envy and resentment, and pays little attention to any positive aspects. The 'death instinct' hypothesis seems to carry with it the implication that aggression is necessarily destructive, and to prevent those who accept the idea from seeing any aspect of positive striving.

As long ago as 1928, Paul Schilder was writing:

It seems to me that the existence of a death impulse is questionable. The impulse towards death may be only the wish for a rebirth in the disguise of erotic strivings. The striving towards the external world, towards grasping and mastering, seems to us so elemental that we cannot look upon it as a derivative of the impulses to self-annihilation.[13]

This point of view is supported by modern ethological opinion, which concludes that, at any rate in animals other than man, aggression has a positive function which tends towards the preservation both of the species and of the individual.

References

1. Klein, Melanie, *Contributions to Psycho-Analysis* (London: Hogarth Press and Institute of Psycho-Analysis, 1950), pp. 276–7.
2. Freud, Sigmund, *Three Essays on the Theory of Sexuality*, trans. Strachey (London: Imago, 1949), p. 36.

3. Jones, Ernest, *Sigmund Freud* (London: Hogarth Press, 1957), vol. III, p. 296.
4. Jones, Ernest, *Sigmund Freud* (London: Hogarth Press, 1955), vol. II, p. 151.
5. Freud, Sigmund, *New Introductory Lectures on Psycho-Analysis* (London: Hogarth Press and Institute of Psycho-Analysis, 1937), p. 139.
6. Freud, Sigmund, *Beyond the Pleasure Principle* (London: Hogarth Press and Institute of Psycho-Analysis, 1948), p. 1.
7. Freud, Sigmund, *Three Essays on the Theory of Sexuality*, trans. Strachey (London: Imago, 1949), p. 60.
8. Freud, Sigmund, *Beyond the Pleasure Principle* (London: Hogarth Press and Institute of Psycho-Analysis, 1948), p. 3.
9. Freud, Sigmund, *Beyond the Pleasure Principle* (London: Hogarth Press and Institute of Psycho-Analysis, 1948), p. 47.
10. Klein, Melanie, *Envy and Gratitude* (London: Tavistock, 1957), p. 5.
11. Klein, Melanie, *Envy and Gratitude* (London: Tavistock, 1957), pp. 4–5.
12. Klein, Melanie, *Our Adult World* (London: Heinemann, 1963), p. 4.
13. Schilder, Paul, *Contributions to Developmental Neuro-Psychiatry* (London: Tavistock, 1964), p. 64.

Two

Is Aggression
an Instinct?

Before turning to the positive function of aggression in the preservation of species we ought, briefly, to direct our attention to the question which forms the title of this chapter. It is a question which we cannot yet fully answer, and which may be the wrong one to ask, yet it must not be avoided, since it is still the subject of controversy.

The concept of instinct is itself in the melting pot. As S. A. Barnett put it in a broadcast talk –

the sharp division of behaviour into 'fixed', or 'innate', or 'instinctive' on the one hand, and 'learned' on the other has now generally been given up; and the term 'learning' itself is coming to be seen as too general and too imprecise to be useful in any rigorous account of behaviour.[1]

Although we cannot give a straightforward and simple answer to the question 'Is aggression an instinct?' what we can say is that, in man, as in other animals, there exists a physiological mechanism which, when stimulated, gives rise both to subjective feelings of anger and also to physical changes which prepare the body for fighting. This mechanism is easily set off, and, like other emotional responses, it is stereotyped and, in this sense, 'instinctive'. Just as one angry cat is very like another angry cat, so one angry man

27

or woman closely resembles another at the level of physiological response; although, of course, the way in which human beings adapt to and control their feelings of rage differs widely according to training.

In a famous book, first published in 1915, W. B. Cannon showed that *Bodily Changes in Pain, Hunger, Fear and Rage* served the function of increasing 'efficiency in physical struggle'.[2] The arousal of emotion, Cannon believed, served the biological purpose of preparing an animal to take action, whether this might be flight in response to fear, or fighting in response to rage. We now know more about physiology than Cannon did; but subsequent research has done nothing to invalidate his original thesis, and his book is still valuable and interesting. When anger is aroused in mammals, there is an increase in pulse rate and blood pressure, together with an increase in the peripheral circulation of the blood, and a rise in the level of blood glucose. The rate of breathing is accelerated, and the muscles of the limbs and trunk become more tensely contracted and less liable to fatigue. At the same time, blood is diverted from the internal organs of the body, and digestion and the movements of the intestine cease, although the flow of acid and the digestive juice tends to be increased. In animals, and possibly also in man, the hair stands on end; and the picture of rage is completed by baring the teeth and the emission of involuntary noises. During anger, there is also a diminution of sensory perception – so that men who are fighting can sustain quite severe injuries without being aware of them.

The mechanism by which these changes in bodily function come about is still incompletely understood. From experiments in animals, it appears that there is a small area at the base of the brain in which the feeling of anger originates, and from which are sent forth the nervous impulses which cause the rise in blood-pressure and other changes which have been outlined above. This small area is called the hypothalamus. The function of the hypothalamus is to coordinate emotional responses, including anger; and, when it is stimulated artificially by electricity, in a cat, for instance, the animal will show all the signs of rage, although there is no barking dog or anything else in the immediate environment which might ordinarily be expected to provoke such a reaction. In the ordinary course of events, the hypothalamus is under the inhibitory control of the cerebral cortex; that is, of that part of the brain which, in terms of evolution, is the most recently developed, and which is particularly extensive and particularly important in human beings. If, however, the cerebral cortex receives the impulse of an external threat such as a fist being shaken in the face, or an insult, it will send down messages to the hypothalamus, releasing it from inhibitory control and stimulating it into action. The physiological consequences are those which have been outlined above; and, once these changes have been initiated, they tend to persist for some time, even though the immediate threat in the environment has been removed. Everyone knows that anger, once thoroughly aroused, takes time to subside; especially if the angry individual is unable to take the strenuous physical action for which his body is now prepared. The way in which the hypothalamus and the cerebral cortex continue to interact so that the immediate response to threat is prolonged is not fully understood. It seems probable that the release of adrenalin, noradrenalin, cortisone and other hormones from the adrenal glands plays an important part. There is evidence that active aggressive emotion is accompanied by an increase in noradrenalin excretion, whereas passive anxiety is associated with an increase in adrenalin output. This was discovered by comparing the physico-chemical

29

state of active ice-hockey players with that of the goal-keeper.[3] These chemical substances are secreted into the blood stream when the hypothalamic mechanism is fired; for the hypothalamus is linked with the adrenal glands by way of the autonomic nervous system. It is partly by means of these hormones that the blood pressure is raised, the heart beat accelerated, and so on; but it is probable that they also reciprocally affect the brain itself. In other words, a circular reaction is set up in such a way that the brain which initiates the emotional response is itself stimulated by the reaction. For our purpose, however, it does not matter that some physiological detail remains obscure. The important point is that the body contains a coordinated physico-chemical system which subserves the emotions and actions which we call aggressive, and that this system is easily brought into action both by the stimulus of threat, and also by frustration. Moreover, because of the way in which the body works, the aggressive response tends to have an all-or-none quality. There are, of course, degrees of anger; but it is important to realize that the aggressive response is not a reflex action which dies down immediately the precipitating threat disappears, as, for example, when a finger touching a hot stove is immediately withdrawn, but a complicated series of physiological changes which, once begun, are prolonged enough to sustain the body in fight or other strenuous action. Under conditions of civilization, it is perhaps easier to arouse aggression than to dispel it; and the man who works out his aggression in violent digging in the garden may seem psychologically naïve, but is displaying physiological wisdom, for he is both giving his rage time to subside and also making some of the physical effort for which his body is now keenly alerted.

The existence of the physiological mechanism is not in

doubt. Self-preservation demands that an animal should carry within it the potential for aggressive action, since the natural world is a place in which hostile threats must be overcome or evaded if life is to continue.

Our physiological discussion has shown that the physical mechanism of aggression, aggressive emotions and behaviour is indeed 'instinctive' in that it is an inborn, automatic possibility which is easily triggered. But need the trigger be pulled? What has not been decided is whether there is any pressing internal need for the mechanism to be brought into use; or whether, if the organism were never threatened, aggressive behaviour would ever be manifested. This question may sound academic, since it is obvious that every animal, including the human, must experience threat during the course of its existence, and must, therefore, respond aggressively from time to time. Nevertheless, if we are to control aggression, it is important to determine whether there is, in animals or humans, an internal accumulation of aggressive tension which needs periodic discharge, or whether the aggressive response is simply a potential which need never be brought into use. If the first supposition is true, what is needed to control aggression is the provision of suitable outlets for aggression. If the latter is true, what is required is the avoidance of all stimuli which might arouse the aggressive response.

Some authors are convinced that there is no essential need for aggressive behaviour ever to be manifested. J. P. Scott, in his book *Aggression*, for example, says:

The important fact is that the chain of causation in every case eventually traces back to the outside. There is no physiological evidence of any spontaneous stimulation for fighting arising within the body. This means that there is no need for fighting, either aggressive or defensive, apart from what happens in the external environment. We may conclude that a person who is fortunate enough to exist in an environment which is without stimulation to fight will not suffer physiological or nervous damage because he never fights. This is a quite different situation from the physiology of eating, where the internal processes of metabolism lead to definite physiological changes which eventually produce hunger and stimulation to eat, without any change in the external environment.

We can also conclude that there is no such thing as a simple 'instinct for fighting', in the sense of an internal driving force which has to be satisfied. There is, however, an internal physiological mechanism which has only to be stimulated to produce fighting. This distinction may not be important in many practical situations, but it leads to a hopeful conclusion regarding the control of aggression. The internal physiological mechanism is dangerous, but it can be kept under control by external means.[4]

Those who are prejudiced in favour of this point of view often quote the experiments of Zing Yang Kuo, who discovered that if a kitten was reared in the same cage with a rat it would accept the rat as a companion and could never afterwards be induced to pursue or kill rats. Kuo concluded that 'The behaviour of an organism is a *passive* affair. How an animal or man will behave in a given moment depends on how it has been brought up and how it is stimulated.'[5] But, as Eibl-Eibesfeldt has remarked, these experiments 'certainly prove that aggressive behaviour can be enhanced or inhibited by experience, but that it has to be learned in order to occur was not shown'. Eibl raised rats in isolation, but discovered that, when another rat of the same species was introduced into the cage, the isolated would attack it 'with the same patterns of threat and fighting used by experienced animals'.[6]

Moreover, electrical stimulation of one area of the brain in cocks can cause a restless searching for an object on which to discharge its aggression; whereas stimulation of

32

another area will make the animal seek objects which release patterns of courtship.[7] In other words, it looks as though aggression is as much an innate drive as sexuality. In both instances, the behaviour which is released by electrical stimulation is appetitive behaviour – that is, the searching for an object which will fulfil the animal's need for expressing its sexuality on the one hand, or its aggression on the other. The conclusions of Scott and Kuo that aggression is learned, rather than an expression of an innate drive, are not supported by these experiments. The fact that the aggressive response requires an outside stimulus to elicit it does not imply that the organism may not need to behave aggressively or obtain satisfaction from so doing.

It is true that aggressive tension cannot yet be portrayed in physiological terms as we might describe hunger; that is, as a state of deprivation which drives the animal to take action to relieve it. But the same is actually true of the sexual instinct; and most people, rightly or wrongly, accept the idea that sex is 'an internal driving force which has to be satisfied'. The full release of sexual tension is generally thought to require a partner, although a modicum of satisfaction can be obtained by masturbation. In other words, just as with aggression, there is an internal physiological mechanism which needs an outside stimulus to fire it off. Although we generally think of sex as driving an animal to seek the stimulus which will bring internal satisfaction, we do not generally think of aggression in the same terms. Yet we cannot define the sense of tension or deprivation which leads to sexual behaviour any more than we can define the possible physiological state which might lead to an animal 'spoiling for a fight' or, at least, needing to make the violent physical efforts for which the body is prepared when the aggressive mechanism is fired.

One interesting fact is that the state of the body in sexual arousal and in aggressive arousal is extremely similar. Kinsey lists fourteen physiological changes which are common to both sexual arousal and anger, and in fact can only discover four physiological changes which are different in the two states of emotion.[8] Moreover, it is not uncommon for one response suddenly to change into the other; which is why quarrelling marital partners often end up in bed together and why some fights end in orgasm. On the basis of their research, Kinsey and his co-workers concluded that

... For those who like the term, it is clear that there is a sexual drive which cannot be satisfied for any large proportion of the population by any sort of social convention. For those who prefer to think in simpler terms of action and reaction, it is a picture of an animal who, however civilized and cultured, continues to respond to the constantly present sexual stimuli, albeit with some physical and social restraints.[9]

We cannot at present rule out the possibility that the same may be true of aggression. Indeed, there is considerable evidence to be found from the study of animal behaviour which suggests that, if an animal is prevented from engaging in the aggressive activity which is normal to it, it will seek out substitute stimuli to release its aggression, just as a man who is deprived of women will turn to other men or to phantasy to release his sexuality.

Lorenz, in his book *On Aggression*,[10] gives as an example the behaviour of cichlid fish. These highly aggressive creatures require hostile territorial neighbours on whom they can vent their aggression. If a pair of cichlids is isolated by removing them from a tank containing other fish, the male will turn his aggression against his own spouse and progeny and will actually destroy them.

There is a great deal of evidence that aggressive tension can be dammed up in exactly the same way as we habitually suppose that sexual tension can be. Heiligenberg, in careful statistical studies, has shown that

When a sufficiently aggressive isolated fish has no opportunity to attack another fish, the percentage of digging in its total of mouth activities is much higher than when it lives among some young fish that it can bite at any time.[11]

It has been proved that the activity called 'digging', which consists in biting into the substrata of the tank, is directly related to the readiness to attack of the individual fish concerned. In other words, digging is a displacement activity which increases in amount when there is no outlet for the fish's normal activity, in exactly the same way as the energetic violence of a man's digging in his garden may increase in intensity when he is angry with his wife but is restraining his desire to attack her.

At the time of writing, it is fashionable for academic psychologists to deride the possibility that man's aggression is an endogenous, instinctive impulse which seeks discharge. Although such writers of course admit that man is an aggressive being, they try to explain all human aggression in terms either of a response to frustration, or else as a learned activity, which, because it is rewarded in terms of possessions, praise or status, is constantly reinforced in human societies as they are at present constituted. Thus Berkowitz, for example, summarizing 'Instinct Conceptions of Aggression' writes as follows:

Since 'spontaneous' animal aggression is a relatively rare occurrence in nature (and there is the possibility that even these infrequent cases may be accounted for by frustrations or prior learning of the utility of hostile behaviour), many ethologists and experimental biologists rule out the possibility of a self-stimulating aggressive system in animals. One important lesson to be derived from these studies is that there is no instinctive drive toward war within man. Theoretically, at least, it is possible to lessen the likelihood of interpersonal conflict by decreasing the occurrence of frustrations and minimizing the gains to be won through aggression.[12]

Such a point of view can only be sustained if a vast amount of evidence from ethological and anthropological studies is neglected; and must surely rest upon the belief or hope that, if only society were better organized or children reared in ways which did not encourage them to be aggressive, men would live in peace with one another, and the millennium would at last be realized. Such beliefs are as old as history, and will be discussed in a later chapter. It is, however, particularly characteristic of modern Americans to hold these opinions, since perennial optimism makes it hard for them to believe that there is anything unpleasant either in the physical world or in human nature which cannot be 'fixed'.

Authors such as Berkowitz and Scott never suggest that the sexual impulse could be abolished or seriously modified by learning or by decreasing the rewards of sexual satisfaction, for, in their minds, sex carries a positive sign, whereas aggression is negatively labelled. Yet, it is probable that when no outside stimulus for aggression exists, men actually seek such stimuli out in much the same way as they do when sexually deprived. At the introspective level, it may be true to say that one deplores getting angry; but the physiological changes which accompany anger give rise to a subjective sense of well-being and of invigorating purpose which in itself is rewarding. Appalling barbarities have been justified in the name of 'righteous wrath'; but there can be no doubt that men enjoy the enlivening effect of being angry when they can justify it, and that they seek out opponents whom they can attack in much the same way that cichlid fish do.

What we still need to know, and what we may hope that physiologists may soon tell us, is the biochemical state underlying tension, whether this be aggressive or sexual. There must be physiological differences between the animal who is in a state of sexual deprivation and the animal who is spoiling for a fight. But there is so far no convincing evidence that the aggressive response is, at a physiological level, any less instinctive than the sexual response; and, provided that the term aggression is not restricted to actual fighting, aggressive expression may be as necessary a part of being a human being as sexual expression.

In the introduction, it was suggested that our use of language revealed the aggressive substructure of even intellectual activity. Once we can bring ourselves to abandon the pleasure principle, it is easy to accept the idea that the achievement of dominance, the overcoming of obstacles, and the mastery of the external world, for all of which aggression is necessary, are as much innate human needs as sexuality or hunger. Scott hoped that, if children could be reared in an environment where there was no stimulation to fight, they would remain peaceful. But as one critic remarked, 'whether such passivity would be at the cost of initiative is an unanswered question'.[13]

References

1. Barnett, S. A., 'Instinct', from *A Few Ideas* (London: B.B.C. Publications, 1964), p. 35.
2. Cannon, W. B., *Bodily Changes in Pain, Hunger, Fear and Rage* (New York: Appleton, 1929).
3. Elmadijan, F., *Symposium on Catecholamines* (Baltimore: Williams & Wilkins, 1959), p. 409.
4. Scott, J. P., *Aggression* (Chicago: University of Chicago Press, 1958).

5. Kuo, Zing Yang, 'Genesis of the Cat's Response to the Rat', from *Instinct* (Princeton: Van Nostrand, 1961), p. 24.
6. Eibl-Eibesfeldt, Irenaus, 'Aggressive Behaviour and Ritualized Fighting in Animals', from Massermann, J. H. (ed.), *Science and Psychoanalysis* (New York: Grune & Stratton, 1963).
7. Von Holst, Erich, and Von Saint Paul, Ursula, 'Electrically Controlled Behavior', *Scientific American*, 1962.
8. Kinsey, Alfred C. *et al.*, *Sexual Behavior in the Human Female* (Philadelphia: Saunders, 1953), p. 704.
9. Kinsey, Alfred C. *et al.*, *Sexual Behavior in the Human Male* (Philadelphia: Saunders, 1948), p. 269.
10. Lorenz, Konrad, *On Aggression* (London: Methuen, 1966).
11. Heiligenberg, Walter, 'A Quantitative Analysis of Digging Movements and their Relationship to Aggressive Behaviour in Cichlids', *Animal Behaviour*, 13, 1, 1965.
12. Berkowitz, Leonard, *Aggression: A Social Psychological Analysis* (New York: McGraw-Hill, 1962), pp. 24–5.
13. McNeil, E. B., 'Psychology and Aggression', *Journal of Conflict Resolution*, 3, 195–239, 1959.

Three

Aggression in
Social Structure

We have earlier suggested that the recognition of aggression as a positive drive which is an essential part of human instinctive equipment has been delayed by the particular way in which Freud's thought happened to develop. His initial emphasis on sexuality, together with his belief that the organism was constantly seeking to rid itself of tension rather than actively searching for stimulation, combined to encourage the view that aggression was nothing but a destructive and negative impulse.

It is obvious that the sexual instinct serves to preserve the species. If the view is accepted that aggression is, equally with sexuality, a basic part of human instinctive equipment, it must be possible to demonstrate that the aggressive drive serves a biological function in terms both of the preservation of the individual and the preservation of the human species. Since, at the time of writing, man is in danger of exterminating himself with the weapons which he has invented, the biological utility of aggression may appear somewhat doubtful: but it will be argued here that it is not only a valuable part of individual human nature, but also an essential ingredient in the structure of society; and that it is only when the aggressive drive becomes blocked or frustrated that it becomes objectionable or dangerous. Whilst

39

the attempt to reduce destructive forms of hostility between human beings is obviously essential, it must also be recognized that it is impossible and indeed undesirable to try to rid ourselves of a part of our nature which is not only innate, but also biologically valuable. That it should be necessary to emphasize this view at all is a reflection upon how far man has come to feel himself alien from the animal kingdom of which he is a member; for there is no possible doubt that, in other animals, aggression, even between members of the same species, has evolved in accordance with the great Darwinian principle of natural selection, and is therefore aimed primarily at preservation rather than destruction. Although it is arguable that man's aggression, under conditions of modern civilization, is no longer adaptive, man could not have survived as a species if he were not an aggressive animal. The aggressive drive has a number of positive functions: and its operation in spacing out the population, in sexual selection, in the defence of the young, and in the creation of order in society will now be discussed.

The behaviour of wild animals is often supposed to be violently and destructively aggressive, so that the jungle is imagined as a place of perpetual carnage. We even use the word 'jungle' when we want to describe sections of human society which are especially ruthless and rapacious. This picture of animal behaviour is actually distorted. Whilst it is of course true that animals destroy each other, killing is only habitual when the relationship between the animals is that of predator to prey. In other words, although animals may kill each other for food, they seldom do so for any other reason. Even the relation between predator and prey is less 'aggressive' than is commonly supposed. At the collective level, predators never exterminate the animals on whom they prey, for to do so would of course endanger their own

40

survival. Moreover, according to Lorenz, the behaviour of an animal which is about to pounce upon one of a different species which it needs for food does not suggest that its hostility is really aroused.

> From many excellent photographs it can be seen that the lion, in the dramatic moment before he springs, is in no way angry. Growling, laying his ears back, and other well-known expressive movements of fighting behaviour are seen in predatory animals only when they are afraid of a wildly resisting prey, and even then the expressions are only suggested.[1]

In fact, animals of dissimilar species usually take little notice of one another, unless one happens to prey upon the other, or unless both species eat the same kind of food, and are therefore competitors in the struggle for survival.

It is obvious that if an animal is competing with another for food, it needs to be aggressive. Since by far the majority of an animal's competitors are members of its own species, it is not surprising to discover that, in nature, aggressive behaviour is predominantly intra-specific rather than interspecific. The real threat to an animal comes from the neighbour of the same kind who wants the same things to eat as itself; not from the alien creature whose needs are quite dissimilar.

It is clear that, in the course of our discussion, we have already reached a paradox. The first basic function of the aggressive drive is to ensure that an animal is able to compete with its fellows in the struggle for survival. One might therefore believe that the natural world was indeed 'red in tooth and claw', and that animals of the same species were eager to destroy each other. If this were so, it is easy to imagine the final state of affairs in any species. The most powerful and aggressive male would exterminate all his rivals and reign supreme in a world containing more food

41

than he could possibly eat – a phantasy not unlike those entertained by human dictators. However, such a state of affairs, although it might preserve the individual tyrant, would be inimical to the preservation of the species. Aggression seems to be both necessary and undesirable at the same time – a Janus aspect which we shall often encounter in our discussion. As we have said, animals of the same species, with the exception of man, very rarely kill each other; and we shall later examine how they manage to be aggressive without being destructive.

Competition for food is not the only area of animal or human behaviour in which aggression plays its part. Fights between male animals are common in the breeding season; and it has been supposed that such fights encourage the survival of the fittest, since only the strongest males, who win fights, gain first access to the females. Some authorities dispute this on the grounds that it is unproven that the strongest males necessarily beget the strongest offspring. But it is surely reasonable to assume, as Darwin did, that sexual rivalry is an example of how natural selection determines that the strongest males shall both survive and have a better opportunity to reproduce. Moreover, the more powerful males are also more effective parents in that they are better able to defend the young which they beget; and are also the most reliable guardians of the community in those social organizations of animals which, like baboons, demand that the adult males shall protect the group from predators. Aggressive competition for females occurs in many species of animals, often producing spectacular fights, of which those between stags are the most familiar, since they have often been filmed. It is rare, however, for the defeated animal to be seriously damaged physically, although he may suffer psychologically. It has been shown, for example, that a snake who has been vanquished by a rival will crawl away and remain sexually inactive for some weeks, whereas his triumphant adversary will, on achieving victory, immediately mate. One cannot fail to be reminded of the Duchess of Marlborough who noted in her diary that 'My lord returned from the war today and pleasured me twice in his top-boots'.

Polygamous animals such as seals and sea-lions defend their harems with extreme tenacity. One consequence of polygamy is that there is bound to be a fair number of superfluous males not allowed to mate since they are driven off by the more powerful overlords. It is interesting to note that there is no evidence that the weaker males are destroyed or seriously injured. Sexual selection of the strongest males is, therefore, a second positive function of the aggressive drive.

A third function of aggression is, again at first sight paradoxically, to ensure peace and order within a community. The phrase 'pecking-order' is now so familiar that it is used, or misused, by journalists. The reason that this term has become established as signifying the existence of a hierarchy of dominance amongst animals, including ourselves, is that the phenomenon was first described amongst hens and ducks in Norway by Schjelderup-Ebbe in 1922.

In any small flock of hens there soon develops a rather firmly fixed hierarchy, in which the top bird normally has the right to peck all the others without being pecked in return and each of the others occupies a place subordinate to hers, usually in a linear series with respect to one another down to the lowest bird, which all may peck without fear of retaliation: [2]

In human society the equivalent to this last bird would be a member of some pariah caste such as the Untouchables of India, which, as George de Vos has pointed out, serve a valuable function in human communities for the discharge of aggressive tension. The creation of a scapegoat cannot, however, be considered the main reason for the fact that many species of animals form hierarchies based on dominance. Washburn and De Vore, writing of baboons, state that 'Although dominance depends ultimately on force, it leads to peace, order and popularity'.[3] A baboon troop, which may vary in size of membership from under twenty to nearly 200, has a well-established dominance hierarchy, in which each male knows his place. The most dominant males often form a separate group of their own, such that if one member of the group is threatened, the others will support him. The establishment of this rank order has more than one advantage for the group as a whole. First, in animals with a good capacity for learning, it ensures that the group pays most attention to the older and more experienced males who may be expected both to lead and to warn most effectively. Second, it prevents fighting within the group itself. The hierarchy ensures that the less dominant will not attack the more dominant; and in those instances when fighting does break out, the most powerful males will generally hasten to stop it. Third, the establishment of a coherent social structure is of value for the survival of the troop in the case of attack by predators. Thus, male baboons will cooperate to repel an enemy; and the way in which they do this is related to the prior establishment of a rank order within the group. Amongst baboons, it is the younger males who form the van or the periphery of the troop, and who first react to a predator, for instance, a leopard. If the threat proves serious, they are joined by more and more of the older and stronger males, until the whole aggressive potential of the troop is mobilized. K. R. L. Hall, writing of baboons, states 'Controlled aggressiveness ... is a valuable survival characteristic in that it ensures protection of the group and group cohesion'.[4]

In the animal kingdom, therefore, aggression is a drive which subserves the interests of the species in which it is manifest; and, although species vary in the amount of inter- and intra-specific aggression which is displayed, the drive is undoubtedly one which is biologically advantageous. It is not yet possible to describe man's aggression in the same kind of terms which ethologists use of animal behaviour; for the simplicity of basic instinctive patterns is overlaid by a complex structure of learned wishes, beliefs, fears and other products of critical cerebration which obscure the most primitive truths about ourselves. Nevertheless, it is possible to discern that, in man as in other animals, aggression serves useful functions, and to see that, if man were not aggressive, he would not be man at all.

In earlier or more primitive forms of society than Western democracy, the aggressive drive may well have had the same function which it performs in other social animals; that of creating a stable society based on dominance. We are used to thinking of human societies in terms of ever-increasingly large aggregations, but it is likely that primitive man was a creature who roamed the earth in comparatively small groups of fifty to sixty persons. Even within historical times, it may be recalled that feudal society was based upon restricted clusters of human beings, each occupying a tiny portion of territory by favour of a feudal overlord who demanded services and produce in exchange for the land which he granted, and who was absolute master of those who owed him allegiance.

Although every society recognizes the need for some kind of leadership, democracy tries to make its leaders as little authoritarian as possible, and by giving each man a vote, and therefore at least a nominal share in the election of government, has attempted to diminish the gap between those who govern and those who are governed. The revolutionary ideology of liberty, equality and fraternity is essentially opposed to an authoritarian, hierarchical structure of society; and innate differences of strength, or even intelligence, between individuals are only grudgingly recognized. Aristocratic societies have a firmly established rank order, originally based upon dominance, though later superseded by inheritance. In such societies, each man knows his place; and the more he is content to regard his lot as ordained by fate, the more stable is the structure of the whole. The aggressive potential of the group is disposed hierarchically in such a way that each man dominates the next below him in rank until the lowliest peasant is reached – and it may be assumed that his aggression is fully engaged in wresting a meagre existence from the land which he is compelled to cultivate. Modern democracies have moved some way from this more primitive pattern, though not so far as most liberal minded persons would like to think. In doing so, they have set themselves a problem in the disposal of aggression. The way in which they have solved this is to allow an opposition – a feature of democracy not tolerated by authoritarian societies. If men are to join together in an egalitarian way as a band of brothers rather than exercising power over one another in a descending scale, they need an opposition, another band holding opposing opinions, against whom they can cooperatively strive. Needless to say, no human society is completely consistent with either the authoritarian or the democratic pattern, but the trend is not difficult to determine, and the consequences which follow are important.

It has long been realized amongst men, as amongst baboons, that if group cohesion is the main objective, democratic principles must go by the board. Even democracies support armies; and military organization is based upon a strict rank order and absolute obedience. The dress of soldiers is misnamed 'uniform'; for, although an officer may garb himself in the same colour as a private, his rank will be emphasized by tabs or badges which indicate that he is far from being uniform in status. The whole of military training is designed to inculcate the notion that men are by no means equal. From the commander-in-chief down to the lowliest private, each man knows his place and must obey his superior without question; and whilst any show of aggression towards authority is severely discouraged, there is a good deal of opportunity for aggressive display towards inferiors, as any man who has experienced the verbal onslaught of a sergeant-major will surely agree. Frederick II of Prussia is said to have insisted that a soldier must fear his officer more than the enemy. As in the case of baboons, this hierarchical structure makes for stability; so that the large aggregations of human beings which make up an army act together as one. It is hardly possible to imagine that the coherence of so extensive a group could be maintained in any other way.

The point of view which has just been put forward is confirmed by the behaviour of countries in time of war. When confronted by the threat of an external enemy, there is a strong tendency for even the most democratic country to abandon some of its liberal principles and to revert to a group structure in which dominance is the most essential feature. The emergence of Churchill in 1940 is a case in point. Distrusted in peacetime because of an exceptionally forceful character which seemed ill-adapted to the problems of peace, he proved to be an uniquely inspiring leader in war just because he was more dominant and more aggressive than any of his fellows. Although opposing voices may still be heard, there is little place in wartime for a formal opposition, which consequently tends to merge with the government in power: and, at the same time, the bulk of even the civilian population willingly submits to authoritarian regulations which would seem irksome in time of peace.

A second and more interesting consequence of external threat is that the barriers which divide men in time of peace tend to disappear. American research has demonstrated that when a group is threatened by disaster such as earthquake or tornado, distinctions of class, creed, age, wealth and position are temporarily suspended, and men cling more closely together than they ever do under peaceful circumstances. Often, indeed, they turn to promiscuous sexuality as a comfort. When the danger is past, the barriers descend once more, and the aggressive component in human nature resumes its normal function of seeking where it may divide. This increase in fraternal feeling may at first sight seem to contradict the principle that in face of external danger men revert to an authoritarian group structure: but the two phenomena are not wholly incompatible. It is likely that the increase in fraternal feeling is most evident in circumstances where the threatened disaster is one about which little can be done, or which calls for no active resistance, as in the case of a tornado or an enemy whose power has proved so overwhelming as to make defeat inevitable. The authoritarian group structure comes more into play in cases in which organized resistance or counter-attack is required. In either case there will be considerable overlap; and what the two reactions have in common is that the aggression which commonly operates between men living together in peace is deflected and redirected in the face of external threat with a consequent increase in fraternal feeling on the one hand, and willingness to submit to authority on the other. Faced with a common enemy, whether this be flood or fire or a human opponent, we become brothers in a way which never obtains in ordinary life. Londoners who are old enough to recall 1940 will remember the increased warmth they both showed towards, and received from, their fellow-men after exposure to a night's bombing; and there are many who look back to the days of the blitz with nostalgia, as is evidenced by the eagerness with which, even after a quarter of a century, they are prepared to recall those sleepless nights and smoking dawns. In Chapter 7 we shall more thoroughly explore two opposing tendencies in human nature – that which causes men to cling together and that which encourages their separation. At any rate, it is not difficult to imagine that, if the Earth were threatened by an attack from Mars, Russia, America and even China would unite to meet it. Nor is there any doubt that, once the Martians were defeated, new tensions and hostilities would once again divide the temporary allies, and new iron curtains descend between them. Human beings possess the capacity for fraternal feeling towards members of their own group because they are able to recognize others who are close to them as being like themselves, and thus to identify with them. It is on this basis that the interest of the one can be submerged in the interest of the group as a whole; and it is also the capacity for identification which makes self-sacrifice possible.

However, the fact that disaster or the threat of a common enemy may temporarily re-direct man's aggression away from his neighbours must not be allowed to obscure the fact that intra-specific aggression is constantly operative in man as it is in other species. The Janus-faced drive has not disappeared; but continues to function amongst groups of men as it has done since time immemorial.

Human Aggression

References

1. Lorenz, Konrad, *On Aggression* (London: Methuen, 1966), p. 19.
2. Wynne-Edwards, V. C., *Animal Dispersion in Relation to Social Behaviour* (Edinburgh: Oliver & Boyd, 1962).
3. Washburn, S. L., and De Vore, Irven, 'The Social Life of Baboons', *Scientific American*, 1961.
4. Hall, K. R. L., 'Aggression in Monkey and Ape Societies', from *The Natural History of Aggression* (London: Academic Press, 1964), p. 62.

Four

Territory and Ritual

Aggression between members of the same species is necessary if the strongest are to be selected and to flourish. Yet aggression must not get out of hand, or else the species would destroy itself. How is this paradox solved in nature? How is it that animals manage to be aggressive without being destructive?

What is needed is a convention or series of conventions in which aggressive threat and display are encouraged, whilst actual slaughter is proscribed; and the study of animal societies reveals that such conventions are ubiquitous. Wynne-Edwards in his recent, important book *Animal Dispersion in Relation to Social Behaviour* has propounded the thesis that all higher animals have evolved societies in which some form of *conventional* competition has been substituted for the direct struggle for food.[1] Indeed, he believes that society, in the sense of a more or less permanent association of neighbours, originated in this way, and goes so far as to define society as 'an organization capable of providing conventional competition'. This should be a sobering thought for those idealists who conceive that society's primary link is that of brotherly love. For what is implied is that society itself has evolved as a defence against aggression; and that animals and men learn to cooperate and communicate because they would destroy each other if they did not.

Of all the conventions which Nature has evolved, that of substituting competition for territory in the place of competition for food is the most ingenious. 'A territory is an area of space, whether of water or earth or air, which an animal or group of animals defends as an exclusive preserve.' [2] Instead of fighting over prey or grazing or fruit, territorial animals compete for portions of real estate which contain the food they require. Many species of fish, birds and mammals are territorial; that is, especially at the start of the breeding-season, they stake out a claim to a particular area, whether this be on a coral reef or in a hedgerow, and defend this area against rivals of the same species. Thus, when a robin comes too close to his neighbour, the owner of the territory will react with a show of aggression which has the effect of repelling the intruder and of defining the boundary which must not be crossed. In the ordinary course of events such aggressive behaviour does not result in the death or injury of the invading animal, which, unlike his human counterpart, is content to heed the warning and depart.

Territoriality has the effect of spacing out the habitat between individuals so that each can secure an adequate share of the available food supply. This dispersion ensures that the population of any given area makes the best possible use of the resources which the area contains. For such an arrangement to work satisfactorily it is not necessary for every territory to be actually fought over, provided the different members of the species can communicate. The way in which communication is effected varies widely from species to species, being visual in some, auditory in others, and by scent or other methods in still others. It has now been shown that most bird-song has a territorial function.

The poetic view that birds sing because they are in love or from simple joie-de-vivre is romantic phantasy. Birdsong is generally produced by adult males and is directed at other males to warn them off. 'I'm the king of the castle, get down you dirty rascal' must surely be the most primitive game in the world.

Territoriality was developed so early in evolutionary history that it has itself become instinctive. Gross reduction of territory amongst wild animals, which occasionally occurs when the automatic devices for regulating the population fail, is one of the very few precipitants of fighting to the death between animals of the same species. This rare occurrence has been observed in the hippopotamus.[3] Man is no longer subject to natural or cultural restrictions upon the increase of his numbers, which is why the population explosion is the most serious threat to his continued existence; but animal populations are in general regulated by various subtle devices which ensure that their number does not increase beyond the capacity of the habitat to support them. Where overcrowding does occur, however, it increases aggression between animals, which may either lead to their fighting each other to the death or else to their succumbing to stress diseases. The latter has been observed under natural conditions, in the case of a certain species of hare which, from time to time, increases its own population too rapidly. The result is that large numbers of the animal succumb to a disease which appears to be the result of stress. Overcrowding is also common in zoos, and may lead to fights to the death, partly because the vanquished animal cannot escape from the victor, and partly because the restriction of the environment leads to an increase of aggression. It has now been demonstrated that confining too many animals in one enclosure causes heart disease, and this has been observed in many species.[4]

In territorial animals, therefore, it may be said that aggression, which originally served the function of ensuring that the animal could compete with its neighbour in the struggle for food, has now come to serve the function of putting a distance between itself and its neighbour: and that animals suffer from something which may be compared to repressed aggression in man if the individual distance between them is reduced.

There can be no doubt that man, also, is a territorial animal. Even in circumstances so far removed from the primitive as contemporary Western civilization, the countryside is demarcated by fences and hedges many of which carry notices stating that 'Trespassers will be prosecuted'; and the entry of our houses by unauthorized persons is resented as much as the loss of any property with which they may abscond. The presence of a stranger in the garden is generally regarded as a threat, or at least as a circumstance requiring investigation; and, on a national scale, the invasion of the homeland by an enemy evokes a more passionately aggressive response than does a battle with the same foe on territory which belongs to neither.

Like other animals, man also reacts badly to overcrowding. Although in advanced civilization, the packing together of people in cities does not necessarily lead to a shortage of food, there are perhaps detectable traces of the aggressiveness which once served to space out both individuals and groups of men. Those of us who live in towns have learned to accommodate ourselves to some degree to the kind of congestion which seems to be an inevitable sequela of urbanization; but, the closer we are packed, the more easily resentful of each other do we tend to become. It is probably on this account that many people find life in cities irritating and exhausting, since they are compelled to control aggressive impulses which arise solely as a result of overcrowding. It is also probable that it is because of the wider spacing between individuals which is usual in the countryside that rural folk are less tense, more neighbourly, and often better mannered than their urban counterparts. When animals of the same species who are not over-crowded fight together, it is rare, as we have said, for them to inflict any serious damage upon one another. Territorial distance is not the only convention which prevents the aggressive drive from getting out of hand. In the fights be-tween animals which serve the purpose of establishing a rank order or of defining a territory, death is so uncommon that Harrison Matthews recently wrote 'It is, indeed, very difficult to find any examples of true overt fighting resulting in the death of the loser among mammals under normal conditions in the wild.'[5]

The great majority of fights between animals are ritual-ized tests of strength, not dangerous battles. Many species have developed 'appeasement gestures', which have the effect of inhibiting any further attack on the part of the stronger animal. These gestures generally take the form of turning away the threatening weapon, whether this be teeth or beak or claws, from the direction of the superior, which is often combined with presenting an especially vulnerable part of the animal's anatomy in the direction of the enemy. Our own practice of shaking hands is a comparable ritual, for we are thereby demonstrating that we are not carrying a weapon. It is generally considered good manners to use the right hand in shaking hands, since this is the hand common-ly used for carrying weapons. Bowing is also an appease-ment gesture, in which we show that we are submissive to the other person and thus disarm his potential aggressive-ness towards us.

Lorenz has listed a number of appeasement gestures in birds, fish and other animals which are of fascinating interest in themselves. What is even more fascinating, however, is that these gestures actually become the foundation of forming bonds between groups of animals. In discussing Wynne-Edwards's concept of territorial competition as a substitute for the direct struggle for food, I suggested that this concept implied that aggression was antecedent to brotherly love, and that society had developed as a defence against aggression between its members. This idea is further borne out by Lorenz's suggestion that appeasement gestures and the rituals derived from them are the foundation of what is known as bond-behaviour between animals. There is no doubt that even quite primitive creatures have the capacity to recognize both their own group and special individuals within it, such as the mate. Since every other member of the same species will elicit the aggressive response from every other, it is obviously necessary first that mates shall not attack each other, and secondly, in gregarious animals, that other members of the same family or group shall not attack each other. One way of ensuring this is to re-direct the aggression of an animal away from its own family towards a hostile neighbour, which is why hostile neighbours are necessary in cichlid fish if their own families are to survive intact. Another way is to make appeasement ceremonies into links between animals so that they recognize as friends those with whom they habitually perform these ceremonies. Lorenz gives as an example the so-called triumph ceremony of geese. This complicated ritual, which consists of a series of expressive movements accompanied by appropriate sounds, binds together both families of geese and also groups of families. In fact a goose might define his friend as 'the goose with whom I share a triumph ceremony'. Men use food, drink and tobacco in much the same way. The man I have a drink with on the way home from the office may not be an intimate friend;

but I am less likely to feel hostile to him than I am to a man with whom I have never shared a pint: whilst the word 'companion' originally means the sharer of bread. Lorenz's other point in discussing bond-behaviour is that it only occurs in animals which are notably aggressive. Animals which form large flocks or shoals are less aggressive than those which defend individual territories. Such animals keep a strictly regulated individual distance from one another – like shoaling fish or starlings – but do not form personal bonds in which individuals are recognized. This once again confirms the suggestion that it is only when intense aggressiveness exists between two individuals that love can arise. Even sex itself does not seem enough to overcome aggression. There has to be some method of either re-directing aggression, or else ritualizing the aggressive drive in such a way that it serves the function of uniting rather than separating individuals.

It has already been suggested that man is a territorial animal, and therefore possesses a great deal of innate hostility towards his neighbour. It would therefore be expected that primitive man, however close his ties to his family and the members of his tribe, would tend to live in a state of perpetual war with other tribes. Such indeed is generally the case. There are, anthropologists report, a few cases of people amongst whom aggressive behaviour and war are relatively rare. Most of these peoples, however, seem to be living under the dominance of neighbouring societies who are more aggressive than themselves, and have simply adopted a form of submissive adaptation in the face of perpetual threat. An expedition from Harvard recently had the opportunity to examine the behaviour of the Kurelu in the heart of New Guinea. These people live in a valley which was only discovered from the air in 1938; and no white man entered this valley until 1954. They can therefore be said to live in a situation which is genuinely 'untouched by civilization' – or at least by our Western form of that doubtful social organization – and their culture is that of the Stone Age. These people live in a state of perpetual war with one another, reminiscent of the blood-feuds in Greece and other parts of the world. However, although war is endemic and almost continuous, and although primitive weapons are used, remarkably few people are actually killed, and the wounding of one of the enemy is generally sufficient to bring an end to the day's fighting. In such a society, although few people may be killed during the course of a year, and war may therefore be said to be somewhat ritualized, a high value is placed upon aggressiveness in males, and the leaders in warfare are given especial respect. In the book in which Kurelu society is described the author says:

A man without valour is *kepu* – a worthless man, a man who has not killed. ... Unless they have strong friends or family, any wives or pigs they may obtain will be taken from them by other men, in the confidence that they will not resist; few kepu men have more than a single wife, and many of them have none.[6]

As Professor Washburn has remarked: 'Throughout most of human history society has depended on young adult males to hunt, to fight, and to maintain the social order with violence.'[7]

References

1. Wynne-Edwards, V. C., *Animal Dispersion in Relation to Social Behaviour* (Edinburgh: Oliver & Boyd, 1962).
2. Ardrey, Robert, *The Territorial Imperative* (London: Collins, 1967), p. 3.
3. Verheyen, R., *Monographie éthologique de l'hippopotame*

(Brussels: Institut des Parcs Nationaux du Congo Belge, Exploration du Parc National Albert, 1954).

4. Carrighar, Sally, *Wild Heritage* (London: Hamish Hamilton, 1965).
5. Matthews, Harrison, 'Overt Fighting in Mammals', from *The Natural History of Aggression* (London: Academic Press, 1964), p. 24.
6. Matthiessen, Peter, *Under the Mountain Wall* (London: Heinemann, 1963), p. 10.
7. Washburn, S. L., 'Conflict in Primate Society', in *Conflict in Society* (London: Ciba Foundation, J. & A. Churchill, 1966), p. 11.

Five

Aggression in Childhood Development

In previous chapters we have discerned something of the manner in which the aggressive drive operates in society. In this chapter we turn to the role of aggression in the development of the individual child within the family.

As we stated in Chapter 1, it is generally accepted amongst psycho-analysts that the infant is potentially aggressive from the time that it is born; and Kleinian analysts especially claim that from the later recollections of children and adults undergoing analysis, they can reconstruct an infant world of phantasy which is full of rage and terror. Hanna Segal, for example, in her *Introduction to the Work of Melanie Klein*, writes as follows: 'A hungry, raging infant, screaming and kicking, phantasies that he is actually attacking the breast, tearing and destroying it, and experiences his own screams which tear him and hurt him as the torn breast attacking him in his own inside.'[1] Since we cannot directly observe what goes on in the mind of an infant, statements like Hanna Segal's are hard to prove. Moreover, it may be argued that, even if the existence of such phantasies about the breast are a legitimate deduction from the material produced by patients in analysis, it may be that these phantasies are exceptional, the products of neurotic people only, or of those who have experienced a particularly frustrating infancy.

The objections to this latter argument are twofold. First, the more we discover about psychopathology, the more do we realize that the borderline between normal and neurotic is indefinably slender. If the existence of an inner world of phantasy in the infant is accepted at all, it is legitimate to assume that the contents of this inner world are much the same for all of us. It is not the presence of the Oedipus complex, the castration complex or any other constellation of mental contents which constitutes neurosis, but rather the way in which these universals are dealt with, and the interrelation between them, which varies from person to person, according to circumstances and constitution. Therefore, if the Kleinian reconstruction of the infant's inner world is accurate, it must follow that we have all experienced violent impulses and phantasies of the kind described, although our way of assimilating, relating to, or integrating these impulses and phantasies differs in accordance with both our actual experience as infants and our hereditary endowment.

The second objection to the argument that the kind of phantasies disinterred by psycho-analysis are exceptional is that it is easy to demonstrate, from legend and myth, that terrifying phantasies of an aggressive kind are so ubiquitous amongst peoples of varying cultures that they cannot possibly be considered exclusive to neurotic or psychotic persons. For example, the figure of the witch who eats children and who threatens the virility of the male occurs in such a variety of guises all over the world that it is obvious that she is an expression of an archetypal phantasy which is common to all mankind. For we have all, as infants, been at the mercy of a female figure possessed of absolute power over us: and although we may hope that, during most of our babyhood, she appeared as tender, protective and compassionate, it is not difficult to recognize that she might also, when angry or rejecting, have taken on a different and more sinister aspect.

When Red Riding Hood visits her grandmother she finds that a wolf has usurped the grandmother's place. The protective, kindly figure has been replaced by a dangerous and destructive creature. It is this *exchange* of figures which makes the story particularly alarming. To encounter a wolf is frightening enough, but to find that one's loving grandmother has turned into this terrifying beast is to add to the situation that basic insecurity which springs from a sudden loss of trust in a person upon whom one relies. When an investigation was made into the effects of television programmes upon children, it was discovered that one of the things which most alarms the young is to find that an apparently 'good' and reliable parent is really a villain. So long as the good and the bad are separated, children can tolerate violence, death and other things which might be expected to disturb them. But to discover that the person one believed was on one's side is actually malign is to enter so unpredictable and unsafe a sphere of experience that children become alarmed; just as an adult might if he discovered that the injections which his doctor was giving him were poisonous rather than therapeutic.

To treat the wolf and the grandmother as opposite facets of the same person may appear nonsensical to some readers. Red Riding Hood does not realize, any more than any other small child can be expected to recognize, that grandmotherly solicitude and kindness which cherish and support the dependent young can, if overdone, turn into possessiveness and overprotection of a kind which prevents the child from developing into a separate person, and therefore threaten to swallow it, as the wolf actually does in the original version of the story. Yet protection and restriction are linked together inextricably; and the very person upon whom the child depends for its safety can easily become a tyrant if the child fails, or is not allowed, to escape from the maternal toils.

The same theme is beautifully illustrated by Humperdinck's opera *Hansel and Gretel*. In the first act, the mother, who cannot give the children enough to eat, punishes them and sends them out into the forest. But the witch who entices them into her gingerbread house is the more dangerous; and the tempting sweets with which she stuffs them are only given to fatten them up for her own delectation. When the children manage to push her into her own oven they free both themselves and all the other children who have succumbed to the witch's spell. The opera is a mythological statement concerning the relation of mothers and children; and the delight which we find in it need not be diminished by the discovery that it is a fable in which a fundamental psychological truth lies half-concealed.

Indeed, we do not have to probe very far to discern the fact that aggression between mother and child is inevitable: and since it makes no sense to assume that aggression, sexuality, or any other drive suddenly appears from nowhere without any precursors, it is perfectly reasonable to suppose that even the new-born have aggressive impulses, in spite of the fact that we cannot enter their phantasy world direct.

However, the kind of phantasies which Mrs Klein and her followers disinter, and of which one example has been quoted, seem too exclusively related to supposed frustration at the breast, and do scant justice to aggression as a positive drive towards separation and independence. We all know that the hungry child from which bottle or breast is prematurely removed will cry and thrash about in frustrated rage. Psychologists anxious to establish the relation between frustration and aggression on a firm statistical basis have measured the time-interval between the removal of the bottle from a baby and the appearance of crying, and have related this numerically to the child's supposed degree of hunger. It is easy to construct experiments which measure frustration, but difficult to demonstrate that, in early infancy, aggression may serve other functions than that of protest.

As soon as the infant becomes capable of crawling, however, it is clearly demonstrating the beginning of an effort to explore and master the external world. As Dr Winnicott has put it: 'At origin, aggressiveness is almost synonymous with activity.'[2] If Freud had been right in supposing that our chief aim is blissful satiation, it would be hard to explain this exploratory behaviour; but if we assume an Adlerian 'striving for superiority', or else an equivalent to the appetitive behaviour of animals seeking for stimulation, the difficulty disappears.

One of the unfortunate features of the human condition is that the natural exploratory behaviour of human infants has to be curtailed, especially in conditions of civilization, where the hazards of traffic, electricity, gas, stairs and many other complex dangers have been added to those which are found in primitive, rural circumstances. We are forced to overprotect our children psychologically, because we live in an artificial environment; and, because small children are ill-equipped to look after themselves when surrounded by the dangerous trappings of civilization, we tend to guard them too carefully in situations where this is not necessary.

In a recent experiment, Eleanor Gibson constructed a

'visual cliff'; that is, a floor which appears to end in a sheer drop, but which is actually safe since the floor continues as a sheet of tough glass. Babies crawl to the apparent edge, but will not venture on to the glass even if encouraged to do so, since they are already aware of the danger of the drop. This is not to say that it is safe to leave a baby on the edge of a real cliff, since the child may turn round and fall off backwards.

The pioneer doctors who started the Peckham Health Centre discovered that quite tiny children could be safely left in the sloping shallow end of a swimming bath. Provided no adult interfered with them, they would teach themselves to swim, exploring the water gradually and never venturing beyond the point at which they began to feel unsafe. Similarly, children would teach themselves to ride bicycles and use gymnasium equipment, and did so more confidently and quickly than if adults tried either to urge them on or warn them to be careful. The American analyst Clara Tompson writes:

Aggression is not necessarily destructive at all. It springs from an innate tendency to grow and master life which seems to be characteristic of all living matter. Only when this life force is obstructed in its development do ingredients of anger, rage, or hate become connected with it.[3]

It is a pity that our culture makes such obstruction inevitable: and one reason why aggressiveness is a problem to modern man is that the natural exploratory urge to grasp and master the environment has perforce to be limited in a way which is bound to cause frustration. There are far too many things which children must not do or must not touch; so that within all of us who have been brought up in Western civilization, especially in urban civilization, there must be reserves of repressed, and therefore dangerous, aggression which originate from the restrictions of early childhood.

The motility of the infant can be looked upon as a germinal assertion of the individual as something separate from the mother, and it is likely that this spontaneous motility is the earliest manifestation of a positive drive. From the moment of birth, each infant is a separate entity, with an individual life of its own. Although helpless and dependent, the baby has within itself, and soon starts to express, its individuality, and the rest of its life will be an increasing affirmation of its uniqueness. As the child becomes more able to fend for itself, so its individual characteristics are more confidently asserted. Every child, if it is to become an adult in its own right, has to escape from dependency: and it does so by a gradually increasing demonstration, both to others and to itself, of its power to master the environment sufficiently to obtain satisfaction for its needs.

The alternation between exploratory behaviour and dependency was beautifully illustrated in a film made by the Harlows of an infant monkey reared with an artificial mother substitute. A young monkey is placed alone in a room with his substitute mother and a number of toys – bricks, balls and the like. At first he is bewildered and scared, so he clings closely to the mother. Then, intrigued by the objects in the room, he ventures away from the mother and perhaps puts a hand on a brick or ball, which moves in response to his touch. Alarmed, he runs back again to the mother; then, comforted by the support he gets, starts his exploration again, this time going a little further from her. As time goes on, he will gradually increase his mastery of the environment, and, provided maternal support continues to be available, will confidently play with the object which originally inspired terror as well as curiosity.

Something like this alternation can be seen in all our children. There is the need to cling to the mother, to be sure of her affection and support. But there is also a drive to explore and master the environment, to act independently. It is easy to see this in a child of three or four. 'Let *me* do it' is a recurrent entreaty in small children; and wise mothers encourage their children to do as much as possible for themselves, however tiresome it may be to wait patiently while the child takes minutes to tie a knot which the adult can tie in seconds.

It is not really surprising that psycho-analysts have disclosed an infant world of phantasy in which aggression plays so large a part, for dependency and aggression are intimately and reciprocally connected. As we shall see when later discussing depression, the more a person remains dependent on others the more aggression will be latent within him. To be dependent on another person is to be in the power of that person; and therefore to feel their power as a restrictive influence which must be overcome. If there were no aggressive drive towards independence, children would grow up into and remain helpless adults so long as anyone could be persuaded to care for them, a fate which actually does befall some individuals who either lack the normal quota of assertiveness or else who have been subjected to regimes of childhood training which makes any kind of self-assertion seem a crime. The infant's world is peopled with giants to be mastered and witches to be overcome just because it is dependent; and so, the further back into the mists of infancy the analyst probes, the more aggression does he discover.

The reciprocal relation between dependency and aggression is one factor which accounts for the particular aggressiveness of the human species. For man, compared with most other animals, is peculiar in the length of time which

67

he takes to develop from birth to maturity, and therefore in the length of time during which he remains dependent. Physical development in man is not complete until the age of twenty-five – that is, until about a third of the total lifespan has passed – whilst psychological development is never finished, and psychological maturity remains an ever-receding goal which, in some sphere or other, continues to elude each one of us. One important function of the aggressive drive is to ensure that the individual members of a species can become sufficiently independent to fend for themselves, and thus, in their time, to become capable of protecting and supporting the young which they beget. It is to be expected, therefore, that the aggressive drive will be particularly marked in a species in which the young are dependent for an unusually protracted period.

The idea that aggression is *only* a response to frustration has given rise to faulty methods of rearing children; for it has been assumed by kindly and liberal persons that, if only children were given enough love and frustrated as little as possible, they would not show any aggression at all. To the surprise of parents who have attempted regimes of maximum indulgence and liberty, the children become emotionally disturbed and often more aggressive than if they had been exposed to firmer discipline. For, if the parents never assert their own rights as individuals, but invariably submit to the wishes of the child, the latter comes to believe either that he is omnipotent, and that his every passing whim must immediately be gratified, or else that all self-assertion is wrong, and that he has no justification at all in seeking satisfaction for himself. In later life, persons whose parents have failed them in this way often show an alternation between two extremes. They either make no emotional claims on other people, or else make such excessive demands that no one can fulfil them. Moreover, the child feels insecure with parents who never themselves show any aggression. How can any child feel sure of a parent's ability to protect it in a potentially dangerous world if that parent never shows any evidence of being able to assert himself or to fight? Of course, a parent who is too dominant may become frightening, and no one would wish to advocate a return to the authoritarian rule of the Victorian *pater familias*. But, if a small child is to feel safe both from external danger and from the threat of his own internal aggressive feelings, he must be convinced that his parents are able to cope both with the world and with himself; and some modern parents are so compliant and so over-anxious not to display any aggression at all that they fail to convince their children that they are competent to deal with either.

The normal disposal of aggression requires opposition. The parent who is too yielding gives the child nothing to come up against, no authority against which to rebel, no justification for the innate urge towards independence. No child can test out his developing strength by swimming in treacle. If there is no one to oppose, the child's aggression tends to become turned inwards against the self so that he pulls his own hair, bites his nails, or becomes depressed and self-reproachful. Often this reaction may alternate with outbursts of senseless rage directed at no one in particular. Normal disposal of aggression is also made more difficult if a child has no brothers and sisters, or little opportunity of playing with contemporaries. As the Harlows have demonstrated with monkeys, relations with contemporaries can to a large degree compensate for inadequate relations with parents.[4] When both are absent, the internal accumulation of aggressive tension becomes extremely difficult to deal with; and the most isolated animal is likely to show both self-destructive behaviour and also rage if anyone approaches it.

Human Aggression

Most of the games which children play have an obvious aggressive content. Cops and robbers, cowboys and Indians, are examples of struggles in which the child, identifying itself with one or other side, is attempting to prove that it has some power in the world, some strength with which it can overcome the obstacles which confront it. Some adults, anxious that their children shall not grow into warmongers, proscribe the use of toy weapons, and discourage games in which mock fighting plays a part. It is arguable that by doing so they are more likely to create the very type of personality which they are concerned to avoid. As Dr Winnicott has said: 'If society is in danger, it is not because of man's aggressiveness but because of the repression of personal aggressiveness in individuals.' [5]

The child's consciousness of its weakness compared with adults compels it to take every opportunity to prove its strength. In adult life it is the strong who least need to assert themselves; but every child has to learn that it will not always remain in the weakest position and that it has at least some strength *vis-à-vis* other people. There is a wide gap between the actual experience of violence and aggression in childhood and its acting out in phantasy. When a father plays with his little son and pretends, falling on the ground, that the son has conquered him, the child recognizes that he has not really overcome the father. Nevertheless, he gets great satisfaction from pretending that he has, and it may be on this basis of phantasy that he gradually builds his confidence.

The divergence between phantasy and reality can be seen quite clearly if the myths and fairy stories on which most of us have been reared are scrutinized. Many of these tales contain acts of violence which, if taken literally, would dismay the most robust; but children lap them up as if they had no disturbing features. Indeed, it is often the case that

70

adults who read the stories aloud are more disturbed by the contents than the child who listens. The more secure a child is in relation to his actual parents, the more is he able to tolerate, and indeed enjoy, aggressive phantasy. It is only when parents or other adults have actually seemed terrifying that the child may fail to distinguish between phantasy and reality, and thus respond with fear to tales of giants and witches. There is little convincing evidence that reading of heroes slaying dragons, or even of gangsters shooting cops, has a disturbing effect upon, or provokes displays of violence in, those children who are not already predisposed; and, whilst we may deplore the vulgarity of 'horror comics', we are not justified in supposing that such reading matter has accounted for murder or other aggressive actions in later life. This is not to deny that an exclusive diet of violent literature and television programmes may give a distorted picture of reality, or have a harmful effect upon those children whose actual experience of the world has been one in which physical violence plays a notable part. In *The Courage of His Convictions*, an habitual criminal describes the environment in which he was reared as follows:

> Violence is in a way like bad language – something that a person like me's been brought up with, something I got used to very early on as part of the daily scene of childhood, you might say. I don't at all recoil from the idea, I don't have a sort of inborn dislike of the thing, like you do. As long as I can remember I've seen violence in use all around me – my mother hitting the children; my brothers and sister all whacking our mother, or other children; the man downstairs bashing his wife and so on.[6]

A child brought up in such circumstances may have his own aggressive impulses reinforced to a minor extent by what he reads or sees; but there is no evidence that the mass media are primarily responsible for delinquency or violent crime, and to forbid a child to watch television or read stories in which violence occurs is a fruitless prohibition more likely to cause anger than to prevent it.

It is the crudity and vulgarity of horror comics, television serials and some pornography which should invoke our condemnation rather than their contents. If we study the content of fairy tales or myths, we shall discover all kinds of horrors from castration to boiling oil. Yet no one seriously supposes that conquerors who boil or castrate their enemies have been influenced to do so by reading the Greek myths or Andrew Lang's collections of fairy tales.

The symbolism of childhood aggression is, and always has been, horrifying; but as I hope to show when discussing pathological aggression in adults, it is only when there is a failure to distinguish between phantasy and reality combined with a persistence of childhood emotional attitudes that the phantasies tend to be translated into fact. The ordinary child may certainly have phantasies of decapitating his mother in her role as witch. It is only the psychopath or the psychotic who takes an axe to do so.

If one examines any typical hero myth, one finds the same kind of story told over and over again. A child or young man, often the youngest or the most deprived of the family, sets out on a journey to make his fortune. He is often ridiculed by his family, who do not recognize his potential. The journey is attended by many dangers, and the hero may find help from supernatural or animal sources. Usually the hero has to kill a monster or perform some dangerous task, often with the object of freeing a lady in distress whom he then wins as bride.

It is reasonable to regard such stories as allegories of the long process of growing-up. The child starts life as the weakest and most helpless person in the family. Giant-like authoritarian fathers may frighten him into submission.

Gorgon-faced mothers may restrict him with their over-protectiveness, turning him to stone when he should be moving forward. When Siegfried breaks Wotan's spear before he discovers Brünnhilde on the fire-girt rock he is dramatizing a step which every boy has to take if he is to become independent of his father and achieve equal status as a male. When Perseus slays Medusa, he is conquering the evil aspect of the mother which can deprive a boy of his masculinity and prevent his further development.

To face life independently is a difficult and dangerous emotional task for mankind because, for so long a period, human children are incapable of doing so. It is not surprising that the phantasy life of small children is full of aggression. They need all the aggressive potential they can muster to protect and assert their developing individuality.

References

1. Segal, Hanna, *Introduction to the Work of Melanie Klein* (London: Heinemann, 1964), p. 2.
2. Winnicott, D. W., 'Aggression in Relation to Emotional Development', in *Collected Papers* (London: Tavistock, 1958), p. 204.
3. Thompson, Clara M., *Interpersonal Psycho-Analysis* (New York: Basic Books, 1964), p. 179.
4. Harlow, Harry F., and Harlow, Margaret K., 'Social Deprivation in Monkeys', *Scientific American*, 1962.
5. Winnicott, D. W., ibid.
6. Parker, Tony, and Allerton, Robert, *The Courage of his Convictions* (London: Hutchinson, 1962), p. 93.

Six

Aggression
in Adult Life

In the last chapter it was averred that considerable aggressiveness was an essential ingredient in the psychology of the child, or else it would be impossible for it to break the ties of dependency, strike out on its own, and achieve personal autonomy and the foundation of a new family. Let us suppose that all this is accomplished, that the child has become an adult, acquired a mate, and embarked upon the venture of parenthood. Now that he is established and independent, with no parental authority against which he need rebel, and fewer restrictions upon his personal freedom, what happens to his aggression? Since dependency and aggression are linked, it might be imagined that where there is no dependency there is no need for aggression, and that if society was entirely composed of independent, mature adults who had all escaped from the toils of childhood, there would be no reason for an aggressive exchange between them.

Many idealistic persons, including psychologists, have sincerely believed that mankind is moving towards such a society. In an earlier chapter, some reference was made to the views of Alfred Adler. It is interesting that the man who based his psychology upon a primary aggressive instinct should have continually modified the terms in which he referred to this instinct, so that the original concept of a 'will to power' becomes transmuted into a 'striving for perfection'. Adler, who in early life was an ardent socialist, believed that human progress was inevitable, and imagined a society of the future in which men would be able to achieve the fullest possible self-development at the same time as being members of a cooperative community. This he referred to as 'an ideal society yet to be developed, which comprises all men, all filled by the common striving for perfection'.[1] We have already had occasion to quote the vision of Melanie Klein, which included the hope that child analysis might become as ubiquitous as school education; but she at least only envisaged a society in which man's aggression would be somewhat modified, whereas Adler clearly believed that 'social interest' can entirely supersede self-interest in human affairs. 'Never,' says Adler, 'can the individual be the goal of the ideal of perfection but only mankind as a cooperating community.'[2] Alfred Adler was, of course, not alone in imagining an ideal society in which cooperation between men would, by some miracle, be substituted for competitive striving. One of the most persistent phantasies which has engaged the imagination of men throughout the centuries is the idea that, in some remote past, or in some near or distant future, there has been, or there will be, an era of perfect peace in which there would be no aggressive manifestations of any kind.

And the cow and the bear shall feed; their young ones shall lie down together; and the lion shall eat straw like the ox. And the sucking child shall play on the hole of the asp, and the weaned child shall put his hand in the cockatrice den. They shall not hurt nor destroy in all thy holy mountain, for the earth shall be full of the knowledge of the Lord, as the waters cover the sea.[3]

Isaiah's vision of the future is matched by a Roman vision

75

of the past; for Ovid, in the *Metamorphoses*, describes a Golden Age, presided over by Saturn, in which 'men used to cultivate good faith and virtue spontaneously without laws'.[4] Only when Saturn had been deposed by Jupiter did this idyllic era come to an end.

The Greek myth of the Isles of the Blessed is closely similar. These seven islands, where all the citizens were beautiful and healthy, were characterized by a total absence of strife or rivalry. Indeed, since all property was held in common, including the women, what possible reason for dissension could exist? Professor Norman Cohn, in his book *The Pursuit of the Millennium*, gives a scholarly and detailed account of these and other egalitarian, communist phantasies which demonstrates that the idea of a world without competition or aggression is not only extremely ancient, but also, when projected into the future, a revolutionary myth which immediately appeals to the oppressed masses. This uncritical acceptance of the idea that society without strife is possible cannot wholly be explained as a wish-fulfilling day-dream compensating for some present state of misery; for it has appealed to intelligent people who are neither poor nor suffering under tyranny. It is, as I hope to demonstrate, an archetypal phantasy; in other words, a mental content which lies dormant in the minds of all men, and which is therefore easily activated by enthusiasts.

If we turn from unadulterated mythology to Utopian visions which claim some closer relation to reality, we discover that their originators are bound to introduce some rather dubious ideas and regulations to ensure that their imagined society remains cohesive. Thus Plato, in *The Republic*, feels compelled to exclude those disturbing individualists, the poets, and advises a general censorship on 'dangerous thoughts'. Others, realizing that in any society some individuals must undertake the more distasteful forms of work, and that being compelled to do so is a likely cause of dissension, have had to modify the vision of egalitarianism by postulating that some men are less equal than others. Thus Aristotle defends slavery on the grounds that there are persons meant by nature to be slaves; whilst the societies imagined by H. G. Wells in *The First Men in the Moon* and Aldous Huxley in *Brave New World* carry this principle to satirical extremes in postulating social orders in which every device of conditioning, education and surgery ensure that each man knows his place and has no disturbing desire to better himself. Bertrand Russell, in *Has Man a Future?*, believes that the abolition of war would result in a decrease of competitive striving, although he does not enlighten us as to why this result should follow.

If the danger of war were removed, there would be a transition period during which men's thoughts and emotions were still moulded by the turbulent past. During this transition period, the full benefit to be expected from the ending of war could not be realized. There would still be an excess of competitive feeling, and the older generation, at least, would not readily adapt their minds to the new world in process of being created.[5]

He goes on to imagine a world in which liberation from the fear of poverty and war 'would cause the human spirit to soar to hitherto undreamt of heights':

There is no reason why imagination should have to take refuge in myth. ... The liberation of the human spirit may be expected to lead to new splendours, new beauties and new sublimities impossible in the cramped and fierce world of the past.

We must all sympathize with Bertrand Russell's passionate detestation of war, and with his efforts to persuade statesmen of its folly. But he is surely naïve in assuming that

77

freedom from want and from the fear of war would increase creativity. A good deal of the world's great literature and music has been produced under the spur of economic necessity or political oppression. In the secure world of 'glory and joy' which Bertrand Russell envisages, it is more likely that creativity would decline than that it would flourish. When Schubert said, 'Often I feel I do not belong to this world at all', he was expressing not only his own internal conflicts, but his distaste for the corrupt and oppressive regime under which he lived. Schubert and his friends belonged to a society which they detested, but which they felt powerless to reform. Instead of initiating revolution, Schubert created a world of the imagination, in part tragic, in part a nostalgic attempt to recapture the simplicity of childhood. If Bertrand Russell's millennium had been substituted for nineteenth-century Austria, would Schubert have felt the same compulsion to create?

Unless some biological mutation alters the whole character of man as a species, it is impossible to believe that there could ever be a society without strife and competition. Man's perennial capacity to imagine Utopia is exceeded only by his recurrent failure to achieve it. This is not to say that strife need necessarily take the form of war and wholesale destruction. Indeed, since the invention of nuclear weapons, it is more than ever essential to find ways in which men can compete and struggle without exterminating themselves or their enemies. But to hope, as Bertrand Russell seems to do, that education could abolish or substantially modify man's tendency towards competitive striving is vain; moreover, if education had the power which Bertrand Russell ascribes to it, it might do more harm than good. For this same aggressive impulse which can lead to strife and violence also underlies man's urge to independence and achievement. Just as a child could not possibly grow up into an independent adult if it were not aggressive, so an adult must needs continue to express at least part of his aggressive potential if he is to maintain his own autonomy.

In the last chapter, it was pointed out that the small child, like the Harlows' monkeys, displayed two alternating tendencies: the first being to cling closely to the mother, and the second being to explore and master the environment. Although, as children grow into adults, this simple alternation is no longer seen in clear-cut form, the dichotomy persists. Man is a social being and, as such, needs the company and support of other humans to sustain him. On the other hand, he also needs to preserve his own identity and to feel himself to be an autonomous individual.

When men form groups, societies and associations, it may be on a basis of common interest or shared background. Clubs, old school societies, and trade associations are examples of loosely knit organizations where the members can be of some use or support to each other, but in which they do not generally become closely involved personally. Other societies are formed on the basis of shared ideals, beliefs or aspirations; for example, religious sects, revolutionary brotherhoods, spiritualists, theosophists, psychoanalytic groups and many others. Societies of this latter kind are bound to contain a high proportion of members who are personally and often passionately involved; since beliefs, whether religious, political or philosophical, constitute a vital part of a man's sense of his own identity. It is in such groups that the opposing tendencies of clinging closely together and splitting can be most clearly detected.

We all, in varying degree, seek the reassurance which comes from discovering other people whom we believe think and feel exactly like ourselves, whether we be Roman Catholics, homosexuals, Freudians or members of the Labour Party. And the more insecure we are, the more do we look for this kind of affirmation of our own identities. If a man is at odds with the particular society in which he lives, he will be more than usually dependent upon forming close ties with a few others of like nature or opinion. The interesting point is that it is just in these societies in which there is a particularly close identification between the individual members that the bitterest disputes arise. As soon as a party line has been established, it is almost certain that dissidents and rebels will appear. The more compelling the ties which unite people, the more violent will be the disagreements which divide them. The history of the early Christian Church is, for example, disfigured by the most violent disputes over doctrine. Men have been tortured and executed because they conceived that Christ was of similar but not identical substance with his father, and that the latter retained an essential superiority. Religious belief, because it touches the deepest needs of human beings, is perhaps the most powerful force which both unites and separates men. An assured system, which claims to explain man and his place in the universe, which postulates a deity who will protect, a heaven which will compensate for earthly disappointment, and which affords the believer a sense that, however humble he may be, he knows the truth, is so valuable a conviction that a man will die for it.

It is, however, a curious and deplorable feature of such beliefs that those who share them are apt to label as heresy the smallest divergence from their own brand of the faith. The religion which exhorts men to love their neighbours as themselves has inspired fanatical hatred and persecution; and although Christians have often been cruel to peoples of entirely different cultures and persuasions, an especial intolerance is reserved for the heretic who professes a faith which is nearly, but not quite, identical with the current orthodoxy.

The same feature is obvious in Communism, which, although not a religion, is certainly a faith. If it were not for the fact that divergence from the party line has so often led to exile, torture or execution, the disputes which rage about 'revisionism' would invite our ridicule. Yet the history, both of religions and political ideologies, clearly shows that beliefs are bound to become modified in the course of time, and that the heresy of one generation may well become the orthodoxy of the next.

The history of the psycho-analytic movement shows once again that men who form a close association based upon a community of ideas cannot avoid passionate controversy. Freud is sometimes accused of having been an autocrat; but he was certainly less dogmatic than many political and religious leaders. Nevertheless, the early years of psychoanalysis were characterized by strife, and Adler, Stekel and Jung, to mention only the most notable figures, all defected from the movement. At the time of writing, psycho-analysts have become a trifle more tolerant of the splits and divergencies of opinion within their own group; but both the Freudian and Jungian associations of analysts have been riven by controversy, although, to the outsider, the difference of view may appear trivial.

The fact is that where associations between men are based upon close identification, splitting is bound to occur, and this splitting is inevitably accompanied by a good deal of aggression. For identification with others involves dependence; and dependence means vulnerability to attack from those upon whom one is dependent. If a man holds beliefs which are unpopular, or belongs to a minority group, or is insecure within himself because of some lack in his childhood background, he will look for people with whom he can identify himself in order to affirm his own identity. But he can only get the reassurance he needs so long as the persons with whom he identifies himself continue to express closely similar beliefs and opinions. Any marked divergence is a threat to his inner security, and produces aggression because it is felt as an attack. Heretics are persecuted because they threaten the security of the believer; and the savage punishments which the orthodox have meted out to those who disagree with them bear witness not to the strength of their faith, but to its vulnerability. The punitive aggression of the orthodox towards the heretic is, of course, only one side of the story. The heretic himself is showing a self-assertive type of aggression towards the group in dissociating himself from them. One of the most difficult problems which human beings have to face is that of maintaining sufficiently close contact with others whilst at the same time preserving autonomy. The heretic is driven to rebellion because he finds his individuality stifled by the orthodoxy of the group. Conformity, based on close identification, at first promises reassurance, but easily becomes a restriction upon freedom to those who need to assert an individual point of view.

The analogy with the small child and its mother is obvious. Where relationships between people are based upon identification and mutual reassurance, there will be an inevitable tendency for splits to occur. Just as the child must needs rebel against even the least authoritarian of parents, so the adult who feels restricted by too close an identification with others will rebel against the confinement which this imposes upon him.

In adult life, the aggressive drive which in childhood enabled the individual to break free of parental domination serves to preserve and define identity. Whenever identity is threatened by too close an identification with others there will be an increase of aggression leading to differentiation. This process is closely analogous to the part aggression plays in territoriality. A certain distance must be maintained between myself and my neighbour or my identity is threatened. But I need my neighbour, for I cannot be fully human in isolation.

Disagreement, controversy, and even competitive striving have a positive function in human existence. For how can a man know who he is, and what he thinks and believes, unless there are others who think and believe differently? In life it is essential that we come up against other people or we cease to exist as individuals. When Eddington, discussing relativity, wrote 'Extension which is not relative to something in the surroundings has no meaning. Imagine yourself alone in the midst of nothingness, and then try to tell me how large you are,'[6] he might have been referring to personality instead of to physical size.

For we define ourselves, psychologically as well as physically, by comparison and differentiation. Colour does not exist except in relation to another colour; personality has no meaning except in relation to other personalities: 'I' cannot function without 'Thou'.

The maintenance of human identity requires opposition, and if 'enemies' do not exist, we are forced to create them. This does not mean that we need to destroy or even to feel vindictive towards those who oppose us. 'Enemies' in the House of Commons are often friends in ordinary life. The same is true of barristers, who, in court, may attack each other verbally with the utmost vigour; but who may, after the case is concluded, dine together in perfect amity. Indeed, there is a closer link between passionate opponents than there is between persons who are indifferent to each other, and the death of someone with whom we have argued violently throughout life is often a sad deprivation.

Utopias in which men did not compete or struggle would be unimaginably tedious: mass associations of indistinguishable nonentities. Man can only be safe from strife when in the womb or in the grave: both fine and private places which we may long for or regret. But in the one the dynamic of life has hardly yet begun, whilst in the other it has disappeared for ever.

References

1. Adler, Alfred, *Superiority and Social Interest* (London: Routledge & Kegan Paul, 1965), p. 40.
2. Adler, Alfred, ibid.
3. The Book of Isaiah, Ch. 11, v. 7–9.
4. Cohn, Norman, *The Pursuit of the Millennium* (London: Secker & Warburg, 1957).
5. Russell, Bertrand, *Has Man a Future?* (London: Allen & Unwin, 1961; Harmondsworth: Penguin, p. 125).
6. Eddington, A. S., *The Nature of the Physical World* (Cambridge: C.U.P., 1928), p. 144.

Seven

Aggression in the Relation Between the Sexes

In our society, everyone is familiar with two cartoon situations. The one depicts an ape-like man with a club dragging off by her hair a conquered female; the other portrays an imposing dominant female giving orders to, or embarrassing, an ineffective-looking male. Variations on these themes have provided more jokes for illustrated magazines than any other, for each reflects a basic human situation.

In most of the higher species of animals, including ourselves, the male is habitually more aggressive than the female. The ritualized struggles which were discussed in an earlier chapter are essentially male phenomena; females do not usually fight each other, either over status or for territory. This is not to deny that females can be aggressive. Where defence of the young is concerned the maximum of female aggression is aroused, and hunters and zoologists know that to approach a mother animal with offspring is highly dangerous. It is also true that female animals can be aggressive to each other when competing for the same male, especially if the male–female relation in the species is predominantly monogamous. Amongst primates the gibbon is distinguished by the permanence and fidelity of his relation to his mate; and female gibbons are reported to be highly jealous and aggressive towards any other female who might become a rival for the male's affections.

In general, however, it seems to be true that aggression in the female is only fully aroused in response to threat, especially if the young are involved: whereas male aggression operates more spontaneously in rivalry, territoriality and display. The administration of male sex hormones to young animals tends to make them more aggressive and, in the human species, the general expectation that little boys will be more boisterous, intransigent and less amenable than their sisters is confirmed by everyday parental experience. Controlled observation of children of nursery-school age shows that boys habitually demonstrate more overt aggression than girls, and this characterization persists beyond childhood into adolescence and adult life.[1] It is probable, moreover, that the greater aggressiveness of the male is biologically advantageous in that its exploratory quality ensures a greater degree of separation from the mother, thereby enabling the male to become sufficiently independent to fend for himself and thence, in time, to found and protect a new family.

The biological difference in both quality and quantity of male and female aggressiveness implies that they are not interchangeable. There is a biologically appropriate way for males to be aggressive and another for the female. This accounts for our deep feeling that the cartoon of the ape-man with the club has something right about it, or at least carries no shameful connotation; whilst the picture of the big female dominating the little man reflects equal discredit upon both. Although we happen to live in a culture and at a time when the roles of the sexes are somewhat ill-defined, it is still true to say that dominance and a touch of ruthlessness in a man are admired, whereas the same qualities manifested in a woman are generally deplored as unfeminine.

It is often argued that this and other psychological differences between men and women are the product of culture and tradition rather than reflecting any biological dissimilarity. And it is true that men and women are so malleable, and possess such a marked capacity for fitting in with whatever role is expected of them, that basic differences become easily obscured by the imitative adoption of whatever family patterns have been instilled in early childhood. Even within a small country like Great Britain, tolerance and expectation of aggression is vastly different between class and class, and between area and area. The man who, in working-class Glasgow, might be considered no more than normally aggressive would, in Belgravia or South Kensington, be regarded as brutish and violent. The 'gentleman', priding himself on his courtesy, control and restraint, is likely to find that, in the docks of London or Liverpool, his reluctance to give physical expression to his aggression will be taken as revealing that he is less than normally masculine. It is easy to demonstrate that cultural differences in the disposal and display of aggression exist. In *The Courage of His Convictions*, for example, an habitual criminal describes his own poverty-stricken background in Shoreditch:

... the only way we knew to answer violence was with violence back again. That was always axiomatic. If somebody sloshed you, you sloshed him; if you weren't big enough, you got somebody else to do it for you. It was as much a part of everyday life and behaviour as the houses, was violence.[2]

At the opposite pole to such a breeding-ground of violent crime are those middle-class households, often professionally Christian, in which aggression is so much taboo that a cross word or a momentary loss of temper is regarded as a crime. Such a milieu not infrequently produces children

87

who are quite unable to stand up for themselves or even compete adequately with their peers.

When cultural differences, even within the same city, are so wide, it is hardly possible to maintain that there is a 'normal' degree of aggression which either men or women could be expected to display. Yet the biological difference remains; and when we come to study the relations between men and women within any particular cultural setting we find that for the male to be relatively more dominant and the female relatively less so makes both for stability of the family and also for sexual happiness between the couple.

We have, in the introduction, already alluded to the fact that the words and phrases we commonly employ in describing intellectual activity are aggressive in tone. In mastering intellectual problems, attacking difficulties, sharpening their wits, or penetrating to the heart of a mystery, men are using, however peaceably, energy which, in the last analysis, is derived from the primitive aggressive drive to gain ascendence over the environment. And it is highly probable that the undoubted superiority of the male sex in intellectual and creative achievement is related to their greater endowment of aggression. It is true that women have often been badly treated by men, deprived of opportunities of education, denigrated, or forced to be unnecessarily subservient. But, even when women have been given the opportunity to cultivate the arts and sciences, remarkably few have produced original work of outstanding quality, and there have been no women of genius comparable to Michelangelo, Beethoven or Goethe. The hypothesis that women, if only given the opportunity and encouragement, would equal or surpass the creative achievements of men is hardly defensible: and it is only those who exalt intellectual creativity above all else who are concerned to demonstrate that women can compete with men in this respect.

Aggression in the Relation Between the Sexes

It is a sad reflection upon our civilization that we should even be concerned with such a problem, for its existence demonstrates our alienation from our own instinctive roots. No doubt it is important that men should reach the stars, or paint the Sistine Chapel or compose nine symphonies. But it is equally vital that we should be cherished and fed, and that we should reproduce ourselves. Women have no need to compete with men; for what they alone can do is the more essential. Love, the bearing of children and the making of a home are creative activities without which we should perish; and only a civilization in which basic values have become distorted would make these sterile comparisons.

In the relation between the sexes, the spermatozoon swims actively, whilst the ovum passively awaits its penetration. The anatomy of the sexual organs itself attests the differentiation of the sexual role; and although culture and ontogenetic development may obscure the psychological dichotomy, anatomy and physiology form the inescapable substratum upon which the emotional difference between the sexes stands firm. In simpler creatures than ourselves, it is possible to stimulate the various drives concurrently or separately. Thus, in cichlids, aggression, fear and sexual behaviour can be elicited by appropriate stimuli, or more than one drive set in motion at once. In female cichlids, aggression inhibits sexuality, whereas fear has no such effect. In male cichlids, aggression and sexuality can march together, but fear prevents the male from exercising his sexual function.

It is dangerous to press the analogy too far; but, in ourselves, the parallel is close. Male sexuality, because of the primitive necessity of pursuit and penetration, does contain an important element of aggressiveness; an element which is both recognized and responded to by the female who yields and submits. Moreover, it is impossible for the male human who is frightened of women either himself to become fully aroused or to awake a corresponding response in the female. Impotence in men, whether partial or complete, is invariably the result of fears which may be, and often are, unconscious.

In women, however, the reverse is more generally true. Although women who suffer from excessive fear of the sexual act may also be frigid, it is the aggressive woman who resents the male and who is unconsciously competing with him who constitutes the commoner problem in our culture. A complete and fully satisfying sexual relationship implies emotional commitment on either side. There are many people who, because of the vicissitudes of their childhood development, are unable to achieve this; who cannot trust themselves to love without reserve, and who cannot trust another to love them unequivocally. The emotional insecurity which underlies this lack of faith in other human beings tends to cause different forms of behaviour in the two sexes. Insecure men are frequently less dominant and aggressive than their more confident counterparts. Insecure women commonly display a greater degree of aggressiveness and competitiveness than their more secure sisters.

Moreover, Christianity has for so long taught us to conceive love in terms of self-sacrifice and gentleness that there are many couples who have never experienced the full splendour of sexuality. Innumerable manuals have instructed husbands to be so restrained, or so careful in their love-making that they have inhibited the aggressive component in sexual congress with the result that their wives cannot fully respond to them, and they themselves fail to gain complete satisfaction.

The role of aggression in the relation between the sexes

may be further underlined by a glance at the so-called sexual deviations. Insecure people who have been unable to achieve complete sexual happiness commonly have sexual phantasies of which they are often deeply ashamed, but which contain, albeit in exaggerated form, the elements of erotic passion which are missing from their actual sexual lives. These phantasies are generally, though not invariably, sado-masochistic in content; that is, concerned with male dominance and female submission in extreme degree. It is significant that there is a difference between the sexes in the type of phantasy which appeals to each. The idea of being seized and borne off by a ruthless male who will wreak his sexual will upon his helpless victim has a universal appeal to the female sex. It is the existence of this phantasy which accounts for the wide popularity of such figures as *The Sheik*, Rhett Butler, or even King Kong. A *frisson* of fear of the more dominant male reinforces rather than inhibits erotic arousal in females; and the phobias of men under the bed or hidden in dark corners which are so common in adolescent girls invariably contain an element of concealed sexual excitement as well as fear. On the other hand, women, however forceful they may actually be, seldom have phantasies of dominating or humiliating men, although they may take part in erotic activities which involve this in order to please the men who demand it of them.

In contrast to women, men very frequently have sexual phantasies in which they behave sadistically; and a vast erotic literature exists in which women are bound, restricted, rendered helpless or beaten. There is generally a wide gap between phantasy and reality, in that men who find themselves the prey of sadistic imaginations seldom actually hurt their partners, whom they wish to enjoy the role of helpless victim. Psychopathic or psychotic persons may act out sadistic phantasies without regard to the feelings of their partners; but most men who are possessed by such thoughts are actually overconsiderate, less demanding and less aggressive than is generally expected of the male.

For those unfamiliar with this area of human experience it is less easy to understand why men also may have masochistic phantasies in which they are at the mercy of dominant females. The explanation is that the regressive wish to be cared for by a powerful figure is common to both sexes. For we all start life as helpless infants, and so both retain the memory, and may pursue the illusion, of an erotic relationship in which we are helpless in the hands of a powerful parent. The female is more prone to regress in this way because of her greater need for a protective figure. It is well recognized that women have a greater need for security than men; that is, for a home in which they can bring up their children, safe in the knowledge that a man will provide and care for them. Men tend to feel restricted by the same situation; caught, and used by the female for her own purposes, and it is of course this difference which accounts for a large part of the battle between the sexes.

And so, the two cartoons turn out to have a psychological significance which illustrates a difference between the sexes which we can take as fundamental. However emancipated a woman may be, she will still, at one level, want the husband to be the dominant partner: whilst the henpecked husband with his more formidable spouse will continue to excite our ridicule, however full of civilized compassion we may think ourselves to be.

As we have already hinted, in Western civilization at the present time, men who consult a psychiatrist on account of emotional problems very commonly show too little aggression, whereas their feminine counterparts often exhibit too much. Of course, this is not invariable. Neurotic disturbances in either sex may be characterized by a pathological exhibition of aggressive behaviour, or else by an equally pathological suppression of aggression resulting in undue submissiveness. Nevertheless, the pattern of the too-compliant male and the over-dominant female is so common that it accounts for a great deal of marital disharmony.

How does this pattern come about: and what light does it throw upon aggression between the sexes? In the long process of growing up, a child gradually emancipates itself from dependence. At the same time it becomes increasingly able to identify itself with adult membership of its own sex. Eventually, if all goes well with emotional development, the child becomes, and feels itself to be, a man or a woman who is capable of competing with other men and women and able to find a sexual partner of equal status and found a new family. As we all know, this process of development is far from smooth in many cases. The insecure child remains tied to the parents and cannot overcome dependency. The father or the mother, or both parents, may, because of their own emotional difficulties, fail to provide an adequate prototype of masculinity and femininity upon which the child can model itself. Rejection, separation, parental strife, and many other factors may render impossible that smooth transition from babyhood to adult life which we should all like to see our children achieve; and a partial failure to reach emotional maturity will, inevitably, be reflected in a partial failure in that touchstone of adulthood, a full relationship with the opposite sex.

Men and women are only fully themselves when related to each other. When such a relation is completely absent, as in the case of bachelors and spinsters, we expect that the isolated person will take on some of the characteristics of the opposite sex. Men living alone very often become fussy,

93

old-maidish and soft: while solitary women exhibit a pseudo-masculine efficiency, a determined practical competence which they might expect or demand from a husband if only they had one. It seems that we all have within us potentialities of being both masculine and feminine: just as we can all be homosexual under certain circumstances. No doubt this is partly genetic; for we all spring originally from a conjunction of male and female cells, and every cell in our body contains chromosomes derived from both sexes. More important still is the fact that nearly all of us have been exposed in early childhood to the influence of both parents. We have learned how father behaves as well as mother, and tried to identify ourselves with him as well as her, so that, when we reach adult status, if we are not related closely to someone of the opposite sex, we have some idea, albeit a distorted one, of being both man and woman in one.

As Jung used to point out, it is characteristic that the woman who appears in the unrelated man and the man who manifests himself in the unrelated woman are of inferior quality. The man whose feminine side does not find itself projected upon a woman will be subject to unpredictable moods and an inferior emotionalism which can be pejoratively termed effeminate. The woman whose masculine aspect is not contained in the lover or husband becomes opinionated and dogmatic, and shows that insecure assertiveness which men find tiresome when they have to work for female executives.

The effect of this lack of proper relation between the sexes is, generally, to make the woman more aggressive and the man less so. Neurotic men complain of their wives' dominance, neurotic women of their husbands' lack of it. In a marriage between such individuals, each plays into the other's hands. The woman, frightened of making a complete relation with a man, protects herself against his dominance by being aggressive. The man, fearful of taking a fully masculine role, chooses a partner who will not demand it of him, then resents the fact that she seems not to evoke his full potential. In such a marriage, each partner will generally show characteristics belonging to the opposite sex and will have failed to demarcate and define their respective roles in a partnership where the boundaries between male and female are blurred rather than accentuated.

This is not necessarily a plea for a return of a Victorian-type marriage in which the female is totally subservient. The emancipation of women is an inescapable fact which will not be altered by artificial attempts to put the clock back. But we are far from having solved the problems created by women's freedom, and for the moment we have to suffer a certain insecurity in Western marriage as a result.

The aggressiveness which is so characteristic of the woman who is unrelated to a man is, as we have indicated, partly an attempt to protect or guard herself against a complete relationship. If it is not safe to let oneself be dominated, it is not possible to be fully feminine. A woman who, because of early fears or insecurities, is frightened of being injured, or of any real intimacy, cannot easily allow a man to penetrate her most private citadel. Her aggression is, therefore, a defence. But there is also another aspect. The nagging, aggressive woman is often unconsciously demanding that which she most fears. By irritating a man, making unreasonable demands and criticizing, she is really trying to evoke a dominant response by attacking him for his lack of virility. Her aggression is fulfilling a double purpose, both protecting against male dominance and, at the same time, demanding it. It is also true that, if one is feeling aggressive, it is reassuring to provoke this in someone else, for it makes one less guilty. Very aggressive women have phantasies of extremely tough men, but marry compliant ones. Insecure, non-aggressive men demand extremely submissive, feminine women and marry dominant ones. The interaction between the two is ultimately unsatisfactory for both, because each is seeking in the other a quality which should have been developed within themselves and which they are frightened of manifesting. The insecure woman is fearful of her submissive, masochistic side, the insecure man of his dominant, sadistic aspect.

We have said more about the aggression shown by neurotic women because it is in them that this is overtly expressed. The neurotic man is, as we have said, less than normally aggressive. This simply means, of course, that his aggression is repressed, and is apt to show itself either in unreasonable bursts of irritability, or else in moods of depression which, as we shall see in a later chapter, are intimately connected with difficulty in handling aggressive feelings.

At this point some discussion must be undertaken of the relation of aggression to hate. As we have said above, aggression is a normal component of sexuality, as indeed it is of any activity in which human beings express themselves. However, it is only when an erotic relationship fails that the aggressive component in love and love itself may turn into hatred.

It is generally recognized that marital quarrels are amongst the most violent of human disputes. So much is this so, that in cases of murder where robbery is not the motive, the prime suspect is invariably the sexual partner of the murdered person. As Morris and Blom-Cooper state in *A Calendar of Murder*: 'In this country murder is overwhelmingly a domestic crime in which men kill their wives, mistresses and children, and women kill their children.' A measure of sympathy is generally extended to the husband who kills his unfaithful wife, or the lover who murders from jealousy; for the '*crime passionel*' touches a chord which vibrates within us all, whereas violent crime for gain evokes no comparable response in the ordinary person.

For the majority of the human race, self-esteem is chiefly rooted in sexuality. A confident belief in one's own masculinity or femininity is a fundamental part of human identity. Those unfortunates who, because of emotional difficulties in their childhood, cannot reach a stage of development in which they feel that, as man or woman, they are both able to love and be loved, are deprived of so basic a source of self-esteem that they are bound to suffer. Some, by feverish competition in the world of power, achieve wealth and status. Others, if the gift is there, translate their disappointment into creative work, and pursue an art or a science with the passion with which other men pursue a woman. The devices by which men and women conceal from themselves and compensate for a sense of failure as a sexual being are so manifold that to catalogue them would require volumes. The normal person, if such exists, constantly renews a sense of value through loving and being loved; and the object of physical passion is thus not only a means whereby the drive of sexuality can be expressed and assuaged, but also a vital source of self-esteem. We cannot escape our physical natures; and a proper pride in oneself as a human being is rooted in the body through which love is given and taken.

The sophisticated intellectual may dispute this on the grounds that, whereas a man or woman might justifiably pride themselves on gifts or achievements which single them out from their fellows, it is irrational to base self-esteem upon an instinctual drive which is common to all men. Any fool can make love, he will argue; whereas only the exceptional person can paint a picture, compose a symphony, or even acquire a fortune or run a successful business. But, if achievements of this kind were in reality the basis of self-esteem, comparatively few human beings would maintain any confidence in themselves at all. As it is, however, the dustman equally with the millionaire may feel himself to be a man, and a suburban housewife possess more feminine confidence than the bluestocking or the lady novelist.

Ideally, every child should have so secure and affectionate a home background that he or she carries within an impregnable conviction of being lovable, as well as the certainty of being able to give love to others. Such a person, it might be imagined, would react to disappointments in love, infidelities, or sexual deprivation with no more than a transient emotional disturbance, secure in the belief that sexual rejection by one partner implied only that the latter was misguided and had failed to recognize the essential excellence of the person who was cast aside. In other words, this hypothetically ideally secure person would feel the irritability which stems from sexual frustration, but would not experience the intense rage which results from a threat to confidence in one's own identity. In reality, however, we are none of us thus confidently secure. Rejection by an actual or potential lover is a threat to self-esteem because most of us are dependent on our sexual partners for recurrent affirmation of our value as lovable human beings. The extent of this dependence varies greatly from person to person. Those who, in childhood, have had the misfortune to be unwanted, disregarded or accidentally deprived will be far more sensitive to later rejections than those who have been blessed with the gifts which follow from an early and complete acceptance by loving parents. But, however fortunate we were in our early environment, we all remain vulnerable to some degree; so that, whenever passionate love makes its unpredictable appearance, passionate hostility is an equal possibility. There are those, of course, who react to rejection in love without apparent hatred. Conventionally, the disappointed lover is a despondent figure, not an angry one. Yet, as we shall see when we come to examine the relation of aggression to depression, the hurt and misery of the rejected cloaks violent feelings of hate towards the person who has cast him off; and the despair and self-denigration which may end in suicide are but a turning against the self of destructive anger which would normally be directed towards the rejecting person.

It is just because love is so important a source of self-esteem that a failure in a love-relation is felt as an attack upon the self. The extreme hatred which is mobilized by rejection is actually self-preservative: an attempt by the rejected person to assert himself in spite of the injury to his pride. And the more dependent a person is upon the love of another to sustain him, the more will he feel threatened and therefore hostile if this love is withdrawn. We have already discussed the relation of aggression to dependency in an earlier chapter. Since man is a social being, and since love requires a partner, we are all dependent upon one another. But it is those who, through emotional insecurity, have remained more than usually dependent who react most violently to sexual rejection. The so-called normal person, who has an inner source of self-esteem derived from parental love, although he will be made hurt and angry by rejection, is capable of recovery and of finding a new partner. It is those who have already felt unwanted or unloved who find any further rejection intolerable, and who may use violence upon themselves or upon the erstwhile partner. The failure of a love-relation is, therefore, inevitably accompanied by hostility, as the melancholy record of the divorce courts bears witness, and it is probable that those

99

who are able to sever a sexual partnership with apparent calm are either concealing their true feelings, or else have had a relationship in which their emotions have not been deeply involved.

References

1. Berkowitz, Leonard, *Aggression: A Social Psychological Analysis* (New York: McGraw-Hill, 1962), p. 268.
2. Parker, Tony, and Allerton, Robert, *The Courage of His Convictions* (London: Hutchinson, 1962), p. 36.

Eight

Aggression in Relation to Depression

In considering aggression so far, emphasis has been laid upon the positive functions which are subserved by this instinctive drive in the life of the ordinary individual, his relation with others, and his relation with society as a whole. This chapter, and the three which follow it, will be more concerned with psychopathology; that is, with those individuals who have developed in such a way that they have been unable to come to terms with their own aggressive drive. In such individuals, aggression is either repressed and turned inwards against the self; or else disowned and attributed to others; or else expressed in explosive and childish forms. In other words, these individuals have been unable to integrate their aggression in a positive way, and can therefore be regarded as mentally ill or maladjusted. No sharp dividing line can be drawn between such individuals and the 'normal' man, since the same psychological mechanisms are operative in both. Nevertheless, it is obvious that in any society there is a large number of persons who differ from the average either in the amount of mental suffering which they themselves experience, or else in the degree of suffering which they inflict upon others. Very often these two aspects are combined, as in the case of a man who commits suicide, thus injuring himself and those who are nearest to him. A complete under-standing of these individuals, which is at present beyond us, would throw light not only upon mental illness, but also upon man's peculiar vindictiveness and cruelty, which, as was indicated in the introduction, are without parallel in other species.

To the layman, the relation of aggressive impulses to de-pression is generally not obvious. Everyone, in some degree, knows what it is to be depressed, however transiently; for no human being can escape disappointment, bereavement or occasional failure in the course of life. Moreover, many people experience moods of sadness or discouragement which appear to come upon them for no discernible exter-nal cause, and which are attributed, sometimes rightly, to physical ill-health, changes in the weather, or other more trivial reasons. To say to such a man that his mood of de-pression was the result of the inhibition or repression of aggressive impulses would be to court incredulity. Yet, if one were to point out that, in a mood of this kind, the per-son suffering it lacked his habitual 'attack' or showed less than his usual mastery of events, it is likely that he would concur.

Depression, perhaps the commonest symptom for which men or women seek psychiatric aid, varies in severity from an ephemeral mood of sadness or loss of vitality to a tor-menting state of hopelessness in which suicide is contem-plated or actually realized. Attempts to codify various forms of depression in terms of severity or precipitating cause have not proved fruitful, since the disorder, like most types of mental disturbance, does not consist of a number of discrete varieties but rather forms a continuing scale ranging from near normality to a condition of mental ill-ness which obviously requires medical intervention. Severe depression is characterized by a mood of sadness, though this is not necessarily the main feature of the condition. There is also a disinclination for activity, which may amount to almost complete immobility, and a retardation of mental processes. Accompanying this is a disturbance of sleep rhythm, generally characterized by early waking; loss of appetite, constipation and loss of muscle tone resulting in a bowed posture, together with a diminution of sexual desire. Many depressed people are convinced that they are suffering from some dread physical disease, although no evidence of cancer, syphilis or tuberculosis can be detected. Those who reveal their mental preoccupations will admit to feelings of hopelessness together with self-reproach, often taking the form of blaming themselves for past misdemeanours of a trivial nature. Some believe that they are the very worst of mankind and heap blame upon themselves, especially for having entertained hostile emotions towards those who are close to them. In Great Britain alone, at least five thousand persons a year successfully commit suicide; and most of them are in the state of mind described above.[1]

Depressive reactions can be triggered not only by loss or failure of a personal kind, but also by the changes in body chemistry which accompany the menopause, infections like influenza, or social factors such as economic depression. These influences, however, act only upon vulnerable personalities and cannot be held entirely responsible.

Although everyone, in varying degree, is liable to depression, since the condition is a normal reaction to loss or defeat, some persons are peculiarly susceptible. Those who suffer from recurrent attacks without a definable, external precipitant are often considered by psychiatrists to be the prey of a constitutional disorder: a so-called endogenous depression. But the adjective endogenous is merely a confession of ignorance, since all that it implies is that the

103

condition of depression takes origin from within the patient, and that the psychiatrist cannot detect any obvious cause for it. A good many people react excessively to comparatively minor defeats, for example, failure in an examination; whilst others become deeply depressed in the face of even more trivial reverses: and a close inquiry into the circumstances and personal relations of the patient will generally disclose some reason for his condition. This is not to deny that persons who are liable to depression are likely to belong to a particular genetic or physical type, but rather to assert that it is not possible to understand depression without taking into account the history of the patient's development within the family, and his relationship with those who are closest to him.

The state of depression is not peculiar to human beings. In an earlier chapter, mention was made of the ritual conflicts between snakes, in which the loser crawls away and is unable to mate, whilst the victor triumphantly copulates. A comparable condition has been observed in geese in response to the accidental loss of a mate. The bird to which this happens becomes apathetic, is relegated to a lowly place in the hierarchy, exhibits a different posture, and also shows behaviour patterns of an unusual kind in which efforts to arouse its aggression prove useless. If and when such a bird is finally able to compete again, he may attack another in a peculiarly violent way, being less restrained by the normal inhibitions against attacking one of his own kind; and after this event, recovery of normal posture and behaviour takes place.

A comparable reaction was not uncommonly observed in patients in mental hospitals suffering from depression, especially in the days before the introduction of antidepressant drugs or electro-convulsive therapy. Nurses learned to notice and report that minor manifestations of aggression, such as complaints about the food or criticism of the staff, often heralded the beginning of recovery in depressed patients. In fact, it is abundantly clear that in both man and other animals depression is accompanied by severe inhibition of the aggressive drive.

Disappointment in love, failure or bereavement are all common precipitants of a depressive reaction in instances in which the external cause is obvious. It may not, however, be clear why the loss of a loved person and defeat in competitive striving produce an equivalent emotional response. In the last chapter, it was pointed out that rejection by a loved person is bound to cause resentment; and it is not difficult to comprehend that failure to gain a particular post or to win some hoped-for success causes bitterness as well as sorrow. On the other hand, the loss by death of a person who has been dear to one might be supposed to produce grief unmixed with aggression. In fact, however, bereavement commonly causes depression which, unlike simple sadness, is characterized by inhibition of the aggressive drive towards the external world and a redirection of this impulse against the self with consequent self-reproach and feelings of unworthiness.

A typical example would be that of a girl who has devotedly nursed her mother through the latter's final illness. Following the mother's death, the girl becomes deeply depressed. Although she may have loved her mother dearly and looked after her with the utmost care, she blames herself for not having behaved better to her mother, and ransacks her memory for instances of irritability or neglect. Instead of priding herself on having been a devoted daughter, she treats herself as if she were a criminal, and may entertain thoughts of suicide on the grounds that so unworthy a person is no longer fit to live. Into this picture various elements enter. First, there is the loss of a person whom the

105

daughter loved; and this loss is obviously responsible for her mood of sadness. Second, there is the loss of someone upon whom she depended, and towards whom she was wont to turn for protection and support. In so far as the daughter is still dependent upon her mother, she will feel resentment at her demise as well as sorrow. Parents who have perforce to leave very young children often find that, upon their return, they are greeted with coldness, indifference or outright anger, instead of the loving welcome they had expected; and this emotional response to deprivation of support persists in all of us in varying degree. Third, there is the suppressed resentment which everyone feels when they have had to be too considerate for too long to someone else. This is especially characteristic in the case of those who have had to look after ill people for any length of time; for the condition of illness both demands that the sufferer be treated with especial consideration, and also may impose considerable restrictions upon those who are looking after him. If a young girl is tied to her mother through many months of sickness, what kind of life is she likely to be achieving for herself? Fourth, there is the loss of a person from whom to differentiate oneself. Anyone, whether loved or hated, to whom one is closely tied, provides a means of affirming one's own uniqueness and a sense of one's own individuality. Hence even the loss of a person with whom one did nothing but quarrel results in depression, for, by such a death, one is deprived of a vital means of relating oneself to another in such a way as to reinforce one's sense of identity.

A short story by Somerset Maugham aptly illustrates the point. Two men have, for many years, been confined in a sanatorium for tuberculosis. They are notoriously habitual enemies; and one plays the violin in such a way as to provoke the other. They are perpetually complaining about one another to the head of the institution, quarrel whenever they meet, and vie with one another about rooms and privileges. Nevertheless, when one dies the other is broken-hearted. Without his enemy he has no one to fight with, no one to oppose, no one against whom to affirm his own identity. The removal of even a hated person blocks that smooth interchange of energy between the individual and the external world which we call living.

It should be clear from the account given above that the loss of a loved person results in the temporary inhibition or suppression of aggressive feelings as well as of loving feelings. It follows from this that the one who is bereaved must, while the loved person was still alive, have found in him or her an object towards whom he felt aggression as well as love. Since, in the Christian tradition, we are trained to believe that we ought only to be loving, we are apt to repress, and therefore not to recognize, the fact that our relation to even the most loved person in our lives is apt to be ambivalent. This is largely because we are used to thinking of aggression as 'bad' rather than regarding it as a drive which is necessary both for gaining mastery over the environment, and for separating us from each other in such a way that we do not remain over-dependent but are distinct individuals. This is not to say that we hate all those we love in the way in which this term is ordinarily used, but rather that there exists within us an aggressive component which serves to define the territorial boundaries of each individual personality which is necessary for survival, and which acts against too great a mutual dependency between those who love each other.

It is, of course, true that not every bereaved person becomes severely depressed. Those who do so, or who suffer more than transient depression as a result of any adverse

107

experience, and more especially those who become depressed for no obvious reason, have in common certain features of personality which require discussion and explanation in terms of childhood development.

In the normal course of events an infant receives sufficient loving care from his mother to incorporate within himself for ever a confident conviction of being lovable. This stands him in good stead in later life; for it means that he will approach other people with a degree of built-in self-esteem, so that, even if he is rejected or meets failure in one form or another, he has something within himself to which he can turn in time of trouble, something which will see him through periods of loss or disappointment. In Pavlovian phraseology he might be said to have been conditioned to expect success, both in respect of achievement and also in terms of personal relations. In psycho-analytical jargon, he could be said to have introjected a good mother (or a good breast), and therefore to carry inside himself an inner source of love which is independent of external vicissitudes. There seems every reason to suppose that self-confidence in later life is based upon the infant's earliest experience of his mother.

Moreover, if this earliest experience has been good enough, it will carry him through the next stage in his infantile development; that is, the stage when he comes to realize that his mother is not only the good provider of food and love, but may also, at times, frustrate him or even seem hostile to him. Since infants react to cold, hunger or neglect by rage and screaming, and since no mother can fulfil an infant's demands immediately or invariably, every infant must necessarily feel intense rage towards his mother at times, and may probably suppose that she is angry with him also. This situation is tolerable provided that it does not occur habitually; that is, provided that the 'good' aspect of the mother outweighs the 'bad'. In adult life it is inevitable and tolerable to feel angry with those one loves at times, and to accept that they may feel angry with one, provided that one is aware of a continuing undercurrent of love, or at least is sure that love will return once the anger has passed.

Suppose, however, that the infant's earliest experience of his mother is such that he has not acquired the conviction of her essential 'goodness'. He will then find it impossible to achieve any conviction of his own essential 'goodness' or lovability, and will possess no inner sense of self-esteem upon which to rely. However successful he may be in later life, he will remain intensely vulnerable to failure, rejection or disappointment, which will seem to him the end of the world, and throw him into profound depression. More especially, he will find it difficult to tolerate anger from those upon whom he is dependent for love, and equally difficult to bear with or admit his own anger with them; for he will not be convinced of a continuing undercurrent of affection, nor expect it to return if love is temporarily overshadowed or withdrawn. In addition, he will find it particularly difficult to become independent of his mother, partly because he will always be looking for the love which she was unable to give him, and partly because it is only on the basis of secure confidence in love that any child can allow his exploratory, aggressive drive to perform its natural function of separating him from his mother. Children who, on social occasions, cling to the mother and are afraid of mixing with the crowd may appear to love their mothers excessively. In fact they are uncertain of her affection and of their own; and therefore, like Harlow's monkeys, have continually to reassure themselves of the mother's actual presence rather than confidently carrying her love with them into the new situation of meeting other people.

In adult life, persons who have received less than their infantile due of love commonly show an undue degree of dependency upon others, and also an unusual capacity for putting themselves in other people's shoes, especially showing sympathy towards those who, like themselves, are depressed or suffering misfortune. This tendency to identify with the underdog gives them the appearance of being more than usually kind, which they often are in fact. Depressives are generally regarded as particularly 'nice' people, able to sympathize with others and share their feelings. In reality, they are not so nice as they appear; for their self-sacrificial tendency, often encouraged by a distorted Christianity in which the commandment might be paraphrased as 'Thou shalt love thy neighbour better than thyself', is only agreeable in moderation. Identification with other people can be so excessive that the person who does it fails to have any separate identity of his own; and apparent sympathy may end in an emotional wallow in which two depressed people feel deeply for each other (and themselves), but are unable to offer each other anything more constructive than a shared conviction of life's essential misery. Moreover, an excessive concern with what the other person is feeling masks a manoeuvre to gain love in a childish fashion. If a person identifies with another to the extent of never disagreeing with him, and sympathizing with his every feeling, he is inviting the other's affection towards him, not as he actually is, but simply as a mirror image of the other's self. This is not love between two separate human beings, who accept each other as different, but a false mutual reassurance based on lack of differentiation.

The conviction of being fundamentally unlovable, so

characteristic of depressive people, does not make a man an agreeable person except superficially. For he will be so hungry for love, and so frightened of appearing assertive or in any way aggressive that he will submerge his own personality in that of the other, and use his capacity for doing this as a kind of blackmail. In the end this manoeuvre defeats its own object, for one cannot love someone who hardly exists in his own right, and excessive sympathy, however welcome temporarily, soon becomes as intensely irritating as frank dependency of which this is a distorted form. Depressed people who do this are actually repeating a pattern from early childhood. Young children are, of course, totally dependent upon their mothers. If they are uncertain of the mother's affection they soon learn to behave in such a way that they could not possibly offend or irritate her; but, on the contrary, are compelled to placate her in order to get what they need. Such children become very sensitive to their mother's moods and feelings; and it is this early and skilful adaptation to her which makes them able to adapt to and identify with others in later life. More robustly confident persons with a greater conviction of their own value are often less sensitive to the feelings of others. On the other hand, when they do become aware of them, they have more to give.

The relation between aggression and depression may be further underlined by reference to D. J. West's recent study *Murder Followed by Suicide*. Of every three murders committed in this country, one is followed by the suicide of the murderer. There could be no clearer demonstration of the truth of Freud's hypothesis that aggression against others and aggression against the self are reciprocally related and to some extent interchangeable. As the author says: 'The intimate connexion between self-destructive and aggressive tendencies emerged clearly from the many incidents in

111

which the offenders' intentions wavered uncertainly between murder and suicide.'[2]

People who are liable to severe depressive reactions find difficulty in personal relations because they are ultimately looking for something which they should have had in infancy from their mothers, and which it is impossible for them to obtain in an adult relationship. Their personalities are formed upon the basis of repressing and defending themselves against the intensely hostile feelings which the scars of infantile deprivation have left. They hate those whom they love since they cannot get from them what they really need, and since they dare not show this hate for fear of losing even that which they have, they turn it inwards against themselves in self-torment and despair. Both the 'normal' aspects of aggression as the drive towards separation and independence, and the abnormal aspect as hate in reaction to frustration, are strongly suppressed, but may burst forth in violent acts of murder or suicide or both. Western civilization has been aptly termed a depressive culture; and the frequency of depressive reactions in the Western world should make us reconsider our methods of child-rearing and our whole attitude to the aggressive drive within us. More primitive peoples suffer from periodic illnesses in which delusions of physical disease are prominent, and which are comparable to depressive episodes in Western peoples. But it seems that the tormenting self-hatred so characteristic of our form of this disorder is generally absent. The price we pay for our kind of culture is a heavy one; and it is probable that the frequency of depression amongst us may be related in part to our failure to meet our children's dependent needs, and to our puritanical insistence that they shall be independent before they are ready for it.

References

1. Carstairs, G. M., *This Island Now* (London: Hogarth Press, 1963; Harmondsworth: Penguin, p. 80).
2. West, D. J., *Murder Followed by Suicide* (London: Heinemann, 1965), p. 150.

Nine

Schizoid Defences
against Hostility

In discussing depressive reactions we concluded that a depressed person was unable to express aggression or hatred towards those that he loved for fear of depriving himself of such affection as he was able to obtain from them. Nevertheless, depressed people retain some concept of being partially lovable, although they feel that they can only obtain what they need from others by being gentle and submissive, thereby reducing their effectiveness and grip upon life. Moreover, they have reached a stage in emotional development in which it is clear to them that love and anger may both emanate from the same person, and that love is obtainable even from a person who can be frustrating or bad-tempered. Although they are over-anxious about provoking anger from those they love, since this throws them into depression, they do not completely divorce loving from being angry. It is anxiety over love being withdrawn which chiefly disturbs them. They repress their own aggression and wish that others would do likewise; because, to them, any show of aggression on either side means the disappearance of loving feelings.

There is another group of persons for whom loving and being loved are even more difficult of achievement. Although, like all of us, they passionately long for love, they

114

have so deep a mistrust of other human beings that any really intimate relation with another appears to them to be dangerous. Such people, called schizoid by psychiatrists, endeavour to maintain their human relations upon a superficial level, or else to withdraw from human contact altogether into an ivory tower of isolation which they defend against love as well as against hate, since these two emotions are, for them, not clearly differentiated.

Everyone, in the course of their existence, will have met a few persons of this kind, whom they will probably regard as cold, aloof and indifferent. Schizoid people of high intelligence often achieve considerable success in the pursuit of power or in the fields of artistic or scientific endeavour. Their detachment from human relationships makes it possible for them to pursue intellectual avocations with the same intensity that more ordinary persons give to the pursuit of love. An air of superiority, so often assumed by schizoid intellectuals, is not endearing to the average person who seeks warmth and comfort from other human beings; and, whilst schizoid people may be admired and respected, they are seldom regarded as lovable. Indeed, it requires unusual perspicacity for anyone to realize that a person who appears indifferent to love is, in fact, especially in need of it; and that a mask of superior detachment conceals an overwhelming hunger for affection.

In order to understand schizoid people, we must venture upon speculation regarding the earliest period of infancy; for, although explanation in these terms is necessarily tentative, there is no other way in which we can make sense out of the schizoid person's character and attitudes to his fellows.

One characteristic of the adult schizoid is a strong desire for power and superiority, combined with an inner feeling of vulnerability and weakness. As we have said, successful

115

schizoid people may actually attain power; but they do not thereby lose their emotional vulnerability, or make closer contact with other people. If they fail to reach a superior position in real life, they continue to hope that they will do so, and lead a secret life of phantasy in which they imagine that they are so powerful as to be invulnerable. In those instances in which reason has been finally overborne, and schizophrenia has supervened upon the schizoid character, it is common to find delusions of absolute power, royal birth or other grandiose imaginations in a person who is in fact so inadequate to life's demands that he has to be cared for in a mental hospital.

In an earlier chapter on 'Aggression in Childhood Development' it was pointed out that man's childhood, compared with that of other animals, is unusually prolonged. Moreover, human babies are, for a protracted period, peculiarly helpless and unable to fend for themselves. In the ordinary course of development, the operation of the aggressive drive towards independence ensures that the child will gradually become more and more competent to master the environment and look after itself. *Pari passu* with this increase in actual power the child will feel an increasing inner sense of its own ability to compete. It will gradually not only become less helpless, but also feel itself to be less helpless. In schizoid people, there is an emotional dislocation of such a kind that, however competent or powerful a man may be in fact, he still feels at the mercy of anyone whom he allows to become emotionally important to him.

For the schizoid person, receiving love which he so much needs is humiliating, or actually dangerous. For, however successful he may be in the external world, he remains so much in need of affection, so vulnerable to its withdrawal, and so dependent upon it, that love from another seems to threaten his independence and masculinity. (This chapter is written as if all schizoid persons were masculine, since this type of character is much commoner in males. There are also schizoid females; but women are generally capable of less emotional detachment than men, which protects them from schizoid disorders, but may be one reason why they tend to achieve less in intellectual and artistic fields.) He is thus faced with a perpetual dilemma. To deny the need for love is to enclose himself in a prison of isolation in which he is likely to be overtaken by a sense of sterile futility. To accept love is to place himself in a position of dependence so humiliating that he feels himself to be despicably weak in relation to the person who is offering it.

We cannot enter into a baby's feelings direct; but it is not difficult to see that the position in which a baby inevitably finds itself is ignominious. What could be more humiliating than to be so much at the mercy of others that one's very existence depends upon their whim? Babies cannot feed themselves, nor move from place to place, nor control their excretory processes, nor protect themselves against injury. Their health, happiness and comfort are, in reality, entirely in the hands of those who care for them. In an earlier chapter we discussed the inevitable frustrations of babies, the reciprocal relation between dependence and aggression, and the phantasy figures of the good and evil mother, exemplified by the kindly grandmother and the wolf, or by the virgin Mary and the witch, which exist in every culture. If the evil aspect of the mother outweighs the good, the child may develop into a person who can never trust another's love, fearing perpetually that she who appears to love him may suddenly change into someone who hates and may destroy him.

Schizoid people carry this anxiety into adult life. Because, one may assume, their dependent need for love has not been met at a stage of their development when this was essential, they conceive of those from whom they receive love as not only more powerful than themselves, a characteristic which they share with depressives, but also as potentially destructive and hostile. Like depressives also, they contain within themselves intensely hostile feelings as a result of emotional deprivation. Instead, however, of turning hostility against themselves as depressives do, they attribute their own hatred to the other person; and when faced with actual aggressiveness from a person who appears to love them (which, as we have said, is inevitable) they retire into an icy coldness and detachment, partly because they fear the destructive power of others, and partly because they fear the results of their own intense hostility. The depressive person fears the withdrawal of love because it threatens his happiness. The schizoid person fears it because it seems to threaten his very existence.

Schizoid people have commonly adopted this method of defence against their hostility in very early childhood. Their conviction of being unlovable is even more extreme than that of the depressive person. They have usually been extremely isolated, with the result that they have not experienced the warm interchange of aggression combined with love which is part and parcel of the development of most children. They are often only children in fact; they are generally only children emotionally, with all the deprivation which this implies.

We have said that schizoid people fear not only the hostility of others, but also their own hostility. This hostility, which may be so repressed that it is hardly recognized, is in fact of terrifying intensity. Withdrawal of love by another, or defeat in competitive striving, produces extreme and vindictive rage, concealed behind a mask of indifference, but liable to show itself indirectly in sarcastic contempt.

Schizoid people are peculiarly susceptible to any criticism which seems to threaten their position of superiority. Everyone resents criticism to some extent; but whereas depressed or 'normal' people can take a certain amount of criticism from those that they love and make use of it, when it is justified, in a constructive way, schizoid people feel attacked and humiliated. Indeed, humiliation is, for them, the ultimate degradation – the humiliation of dependency, the humiliation of defeat, even the humiliation of receiving instead of giving. It is difficult for schizoid people to accept anything from others without feeling denigrated by the gift, which is why they so often bite the hands that feed them.

A brilliant delineation of such a character can be found in *The Quest for Corvo*.[1] Frederick Rolfe, the subject of this book, showed in extreme form all the schizoid characteristics which have so far been discussed. His most successful book, *Hadrian the Seventh*,[2] is a phantasy of his own elevation to the papacy. But he was quite unable to receive help or affection without feeling humiliated by it; and his letters to publishers and friends who supported him are replete with vindictiveness and contempt. The schizoid adaptation of isolation and superiority is threatened by being placed in the receptive position. Needing so much, they give the appearance of needing nothing, and of resenting what is offered them.

It is, of course, only those with whom they become emotionally involved or upon whom they are financially dependent who have the power to hurt them or to make them feel humiliated. The majority of the human race have little meaning for them. Like Freud, who admitted as much in one of his letters, they regard the general run of human beings as trash.

In schizoid characters who are less obviously disturbed

than Frederick Rolfe, politeness and a concern for the feelings of others which may even be tender keep other people at arm's length. The stiff upper lip, the persona of the English gentleman, is a particularly appropriate mask for the schizoid person to adopt. Good manners, self-control, consideration for others and self-reliance are all admirable qualities or modes of behaviour. Each, however, can be adopted as a defence against becoming involved with another person at any deep emotional level. For when it comes to loving and hating, good manners count for nothing; self-control can inhibit the sexual relation, self-reliance be a denial of the need for another's love, consideration for the other's feeling merely a device to avoid provocation.

The disposal of aggression is particularly difficult for schizoid people; for, in them, the normal, positive aspects of aggression in defining identity and asserting independence are so intermingled with hatred for past disregard that it is almost impossible for them to be aggressive without being destructive. When rebuff or criticism, however mild, are interpreted as insult, withdrawal or murder may seem the only possible alternatives.

So long as these defences are maintained, schizoid people may, as we have said, be notably successful. Some leaders of an apocalyptic, visionary type belong to this category: and attain power because they identify their own desire for it with the cause that they espouse. A defeated or humiliated country will rally to a leader who, in seeking the restoration of past glory, believes himself to personify the fatherland. A contemporary example is General de Gaulle, who from his earliest years had phantasies of being, like Joan of Arc, his country's saviour, who shows little interest in human relationships, is notoriously touchy and difficult; and who openly identifies himself with France and '*la gloire*' which should pertain to both. The general has so far remained sane; but it is not unlikely that old age and the deterioration consequent upon cerebral arteriosclerosis might undermine his defences and release paranoid ideas and behaviour. This remarkable leader could, like Stalin, become a danger both to his country and to the world in a manner which is unlikely in the case of political leaders of more conventional mould. If there is one lesson to be learned from history it is that men should beware of giving power to visionaries. They are safer with the shrewd, practical men of affairs who constitute the majority of politicians.

The most fruitful consequence of the schizoid character is found in the field of creative endeavour. Indeed, some of the world's greatest art, philosophy and science take origin from this type of emotional laming. Karl Stern, in his book *The Flight from Woman*,[3] has demonstrated that, in the case of philosophers like Descartes and Schopenhauer, it is their very alienation from love which has given birth to their philosophies. The detachment and objectivity so necessary for a philosopher, and the need to create an ideal world to compensate for the disappointments of reality, have their roots in maternal deprivation. The disorder of unruly and destructive emotion is subdued by the construction of a universe in which order and harmony predominate; and the conviction of inner weakness disproven by the power of creation, which manifests itself in the productions of the pen, if not in human relationships. Beethoven, for example, showed many schizoid traits. He was generally morose and suspicious, and never succeeded in making any permanent relationship with a woman. His deafness increased his isolation and mistrust of human beings; but this disability merely accentuated characteristics which were already present. He displayed, in marked degree, the conviction of superiority so typical of schizoid

121

characters; being, as Michael Hamburger remarks, 'the first composer to claim the prerogatives of genius'.[4] In personal relations he was so touchy that even his closest friends were liable to find themselves excluded on account of some supposed slight: whilst his relations with publishers were almost as stormy as those of Frederick Rolfe. In compensation for his disappointment with, and resentment of, actual human beings, Beethoven imagined an ideal world of love and friendship. It is no accident that he chose to end his last symphony with Schiller's 'Ode to Joy', with its emphasis upon brotherly love. His music, perhaps more obviously than that of any other composer, displays considerable aggression in the sense of power, forcefulness and strength. It is easy to imagine that, had he not been able to sublimate his hostility in his music, he might well have succumbed to a paranoid psychosis, as in fact quite a number of deaf persons do. As he said himself, 'All that is called life shall be sacrificed to sublime Art, a sacrament of Art'.[5] It is one of the most remarkable features of the human condition that such a sacrifice can be even partially successful.

The man with a fully-developed schizoid character is clearly different from the common run, even if he is not a creative genius. Yet it is important to realize that schizoid potentialities lie latent within us all, and that we all, on occasion, employ the same methods of defence against our hostile emotions as does the schizoid person habitually. For we are all, to some degree, sensitive to slight or humiliation. We must all carry within us infantile memories of being helpless and disregarded; and at times most of us feel so hostile to those we love that we make use of the mechanism of withdrawal into isolation. Moreover, if sublimation and the symbolic expression of hostility were impossible to man we should be even more destructive than we are.

In the next chapter we shall consider what happens to

man's hostility when his defences break down, or when he
has never reached a stage of emotional development in
which he can make use of the techniques of dealing with
hate so far described.

References

1. Symons, A. J. A., *The Quest for Corvo* (London: Cassell, 1955;
   Harmondsworth: Penguin).
2. Rolfe, Frederick, *Hadrian the Seventh* (London: Chatto &
   Windus, 1954; Harmondsworth: Penguin).
3. Stern, Karl, *The Flight from Woman* (London: Allen & Unwin,
   1966).
4. Hamburger, Michael, *Beethoven: Letters, Journal and Conversa-
   tions* (London: Jonathan Cape, 1966), p. 3.
5. Hamburger, Michael, ibid., p. 135.

Ten

Paranoid
Hostility

In this chapter an attempt will be made to give an explanation of man's unique capacity for cruelty.

In our brief review of aggression in other species, we concluded that even animals which prey upon one another do not rejoice in cruelty for its own sake. The cat, playing with the mouse before it suddenly kills it, is behaving as it would with any small moving object which gives an opportunity of exercising its skill in catching and pouncing. It is inconceivable that a cat could so identify itself with a mouse as to enjoy the latter's fear. Yet men, with hatred in their hearts, take pleasure in prolonging the agonies of helpless victims, and show extreme ingenuity in devising tortures which cause the maximum pain and the minimum risk of a quick ending. The relation of predator to prey cannot be called sadistic, without robbing the adjective of its meaning; for the enjoyment of another's pain is, so far as one can tell, peculiar to human beings.

As we have seen, moreover, when an animal attacks another of the same species, it is generally content to prove its superior strength without proceeding to maim or seriously injure its opponent. Except in the special circumstances of overcrowding or actual shortage of food, most intra-specific struggles are ritualized tests of strength. The defeated animal is allowed to retreat and is not pursued: the victor is satisfied with proof of status and with the demonstration that he can defend his family and territory. But man is not content to let his victim escape. He may, and often does, go on to inflict such humiliation and pain that his defeated enemy longs for death. The cruelty of animals is largely a myth: the cruelty of man is a grim reality.

Indeed, it seems that, for man, there is something about weakness or defeat which actually increases hostility. In Chapter 4 we discussed appeasement gestures in animals: the devices by which a defeated animal shows that it concedes victory to its opponent, usually by presenting a vulnerable part of its anatomy to the foe, or by turning away its own aggressive weapons. Man displays appeasement gestures also; but the curious and distressing fact is that these often fail to have any effect. No amount of bowing, smiling or kneeling by the defeated enemy would have been likely to assuage the wrath of Basil the Second, the conqueror of the Bulgarians. According to Gibbon –

His cruelty inflicted a cool and exquisite vengeance on fifteen thousand captives who had been guilty of the defence of their country; they were deprived of sight; but to one of each hundred a single eye was left, that he might conduct his blind century to the presence of their king.[1]

Nor can it be supposed that the persecution of the weak is the prerogative of barbarous monarchs. It is surely one of the most curious features of the human condition that advanced countries like Great Britain require a National Society for the Prevention of Cruelty to Children. Although animals may forcibly reprove or restrain their young or even, under certain circumstances, eat them, it is hard to imagine any animal deliberately beating its offspring to death. Yet human beings not infrequently inflict appalling

125

injuries upon their own progeny. In one year alone, the N.S.P.C.C. saw 114,641 children; and, although the organization is reluctant to take legal action where this can be avoided, there were 39,223 cases in which parents had to appear in court.[2]

It is impossible to refrain from the conclusion that, in human beings, a show of weakness on the part of the defeated is as likely to increase hatred as to restrain it. Perhaps our most unpleasant characteristic as a species is our proclivity for bullying the helpless.

The use of the word 'hatred' rather than 'aggression' in the last paragraph is deliberate. Throughout most of this book emphasis has been laid upon the positive aspects of the aggressive drive, since these have been largely ignored by contemporary psychology. But the relation of aggression to hate was briefly touched upon in the chapter on aggression in the relation between the sexes, in the chapter on depression, and again in the chapter on schizoid defences. Aggression turns to hatred when it comes to contain an admixture of revenge; and the tendency to persecute those who are already defeated, or who are obviously weaker than the aggressor, can only be explained by the latter's need to revenge himself for past humiliations.

It is the failure to distinguish between aggression and hatred which has led naïve, liberal humanists to label all aggression as 'bad', and which has also led them to hold the ridiculous belief that, if human beings were never frustrated, they would not be aggressive at all.

It is, of course, obvious that frustration increases aggression. Indeed, even frustration has its positive aspects. When our drive to master the environment, or take from it what we need, is obstructed, we become angry; and our anger increases our power to overcome the obstacle. The tree which blocks our path, and which is just too heavy for us to lift when we are placid, evokes our anger and puts us into the best physiological condition for making our strongest muscular efforts. The woman who resists a man's sexual advances arouses more aggression within him; and this increase in male dominance may enable him to overcome her resistance and obtain satisfaction for his desire. But, as our study of the positive functions of aggression has amply demonstrated, the hypothesis that all aggression can be explained as a response to frustration cannot possibly be true. When, however, we turn to examine hatred, frustration, past or present, plays a much more important part.

In ordinary day-to-day existence a modicum of introspection will often reveal the point at which aggression becomes hate. We all have, and need, opponents; and, even within our own families, there are bound to be perpetual struggles for dominance. Sometimes our will prevails, and sometimes that of the other who is opposing us: and we accept this interchange as a normal part of life. There can be few parents, however, who have not sometimes punished a child in a way inappropriately severe for a particular offence; and who have not later realized with some shame that they were 'taking it out on' the child, either because of the latter's past misdeeds, or else as a result of other, personal frustrations which may have nothing to do with the child at all. It is at the point at which 'taking it out on' someone supervenes that aggression is liable to turn into hatred. Indeed, the colloquial phrase 'taking it out on' implies that there is an 'it' within the person – perhaps a chronic state of irritability – which causes an angry response inappropriate to the actual situation. It may seem absurd to choose such an inconsiderable and homely example to illustrate the relation between aggression and hate; and many parents will probably deny that they ever hate their children, even if they admit that they have sometimes 'taken it out on' them. Nevertheless, this illustration depicts two facts about human nature which go far to explain why men, unlike animals, are likely to behave with cruelty towards the defeated and the weak.

The first is man's liability to react to present situations in terms of the past. Animals also do this, since if they could not, they would hardly be able to learn from past experience. But in man the capacity of memory is fantastically developed. It is not only man's prolonged infancy which distinguishes him from other animals; it is also the size and complexity of his brain. Although it is justifiable to question the accuracy of the earliest memories which are disinterred by psycho-analysts, there can be no doubt that we are shaped by the experience of our infancy. As the anthropologist, Professor Washburn, said at a recent symposium:

We can now say that there is no question that the earliest events in life, in the first year or two, are profoundly important, whether for a young rhesus monkey or a human being. This is not something which is generally recognized around the world; infants are frequently treated with the greatest casualness.[3]

The 'it' which we are likely to 'take out' on others may be our frustrated anger following a bad day at work; or it may be something less easily purged, echoes of humiliation and disappointment from our earliest, most helpless days. We like to think of babies as responsive, smiling, happy creatures, and to forget their tears and helpless rages. In the last chapter, we saw that schizoid people defend themselves by withdrawal from emotional contact against the expression of intensely hostile feelings which they carry with them into adult life as a result of an unfavourable early environment. It would be a misuse of a useful term to label all human beings as schizoid: yet there can be little doubt that, because of our prolonged dependency as infants and children,

128

and our consequent vulnerability to humiliation and disregard, we all contain within us, in varying degree, impulses of hate and revenge which have a vindictive quality that is absent from 'normal' aggression.

For the curve of man's growth and development is in fact different from that of other animals. A human infant is particularly helpless at birth, and dependent on the mother for longer in proportion to its total life-span than other primates. In addition to this, however, growth and development, which progress rapidly to the age of about five, slow down at this point, and do not regain momentum until just before puberty.[4] Psychologists have rightly concentrated much attention upon the early relationship of the infant with its mother. This later period of less rapid growth, roughly corresponding to Freud's 'latency period', is also extremely important: and many of man's peculiarities are as much related to his lengthened childhood as to the prolongation of his dependency in infancy. Not all these peculiarities are as distasteful as his tendency towards cruelty. The development of conceptual thought, symbolization, the power to create, and man's astounding adaptability and flexibility, are all consequences of his delayed maturation.

A second feature in which we appear to be different from other animals is in our capacity for projection. By projection is meant the tendency to attribute to other persons emotions, ideas, or attitudes which they do not in fact possess, but which take origin within ourselves. Almost any characteristic can be projected upon another. Persons in love habitually project an ideal of the opposite sex upon one another; political leaders often receive projections of authoritative wisdom which they seldom deserve; analysts are commonly regarded as infinitely understanding parents, priests as spiritual beings superior to the desires of the flesh.

In this context, however, we are chiefly concerned with what is generally known as paranoid projection: that is, with the attribution to others of malignant hostility.

In clear-cut form, this is best seen in the mental illness known as paranoid schizophrenia. Those who have succumbed to this condition have been unable, like schizoid persons, to deal with their own hostility by withdrawal. Instead they attribute it to other people, and believe themselves to be the subject of unwarranted persecution. In some instances, the imagined persecutors are a comparatively small group; freemasons, Jews, Negroes or merely the subject's own family. In others, the whole world seems to be set against him, so that he cannot go out into the street without feeling that people are talking about him, that casual passers-by are regarding him with contempt, and that he is the object of malicious attention from total strangers.

Paranoid schizophrenia is not infrequently ushered in by phantasies or dreams that the whole world is about to be destroyed, an illusion which reflects the subject's own intense hostility to a world which he feels has rejected him, but which also contains a truth, since his own, subjective world is indeed collapsing in ruins. There is generally some attempt to maintain self-esteem by grandiose phantasies. To be the subject of widespread attention, even if this be malicious, implies that one must be a person of consequence. Paranoid schizophrenics feel that they are themselves powerless to resist the evil intentions of others, especially since their persecutors are often imagined to possess telepathic, hypnotic or supernatural powers. At the same time, they conceive themselves to be extremely important. This paradox echoes the earliest state of infancy, in which the baby, although helplessly dependent, is also the centre of the household and the person whose imperious needs are paramount.

It is no accident that, prior to the development of frank insanity, many schizophrenics have been regarded as unusually quiet, retiring people displaying less than the normal quota of aggression. For, in them, the aggressive drive towards self-assertion has been blocked at an extremely early stage in their development, with the result that almost the whole of their aggressive potential has turned to hate against a world which appears to have frustrated them from early childhood onwards.

It is fortunate that paranoid schizophrenics are seldom effective enough in life to gain positions of power, since their readiness to descry hostility where none exists, and their desire for revenge, makes them potentially dangerous. A certain number of murders are in fact committed by paranoid schizophrenics; but the majority are unable to express their hostility except in phantasy. As we have seen, however, the risk of schizophrenia supervening upon the schizoid character is a real one; and schizoid people, although unhappy, are often successful.

Although most obvious in the insane, the capacity for paranoid projection is, regrettably, not confined to them. Indeed, we must assume that the whole of mankind possesses some underlying paranoid potential. When discussing depression, it was indicated that most people, at least in our culture, know what it is to be depressed: but depression is, in nearly every instance, a transient condition from which, whether mild or severe, the majority of persons recover. The tendency towards paranoid projection, though more deeply buried in 'normal' people, is far less intermittent and even more ubiquitous than the tendency towards depression.

In primitive cultures, for example, physical illness is seldom attributed to the internal malfunction of the subject's own body. Instead, he believes that he has been poisoned or

131

bewitched, and conceives that his disorder is the result of deliberate malice on the part of another person. As we have already indicated, depression is rare amongst primitive peoples; but acute psychotic episodes in which paranoid projections are evident and murder is frequent are much commoner than in Western cultures.

It is also obvious that many cultures maintain, and perhaps require, sub-groups who are the recipients of paranoid projections, and who are treated with hostility and contempt. The untouchables of India and the outcasts of Japan are examples of groups of human beings considered as polluted and potentially contaminating. It is true that these groups are not obviously conceived of as powerful in a conventional sense. Nevertheless, their continued association with dirt and excrement is often linked with the supernatural; and the care with which the society segregates them demonstrates its fear of their power to cause pollution.

If we consider more familiar forms of intolerance, the paradox by which a scapegoat minority, although in reality weak, can be regarded as potentially powerful becomes more obvious. In Nazi Germany, Jews were not only regarded as despicable outcasts. It was also widely believed that there was a Jewish world conspiracy which was plotting to undermine the existing state and achieve supreme power. In his book *Warrant for Genocide*,[5] Norman Cohn has amply demonstrated that the most absurd phantasies about Jews have been taken for truth by very large numbers of ordinary people, and that, although the mass extermination of the Jews by the Nazis is an unparalleled example of man's inhumanity to man, the readiness with which massive sections of a community will project images of evil persecutors upon an innocent minority is a recurrent historical phenomenon.

Jews were not only accused of financial rapacity and of aiming at world power: they were also slandered as child-murderers and poisoners, historically repetitive calumnies which are of interest psychologically, since schizophrenics not infrequently accuse their parents of trying to murder or poison them. The absurdity of these accusations was, in Nazi Germany, matched by the equally ridiculous idealization of the so-called 'Aryan' race. The schizoid tendency to split human beings into ideally good and 'ideally' bad was never more obvious.

It might be expected that, when men finally capture the individuals upon whom they have projected images of evil, they would discard their illusions and see their imagined persecutors as no more powerful nor more wicked than themselves. Yet, as we know both from the medieval witch-trials and from the concentration camps, this is far from being the case. The abominable cruelties which have been inflicted upon many thousands of men, women and children attest the relish with which the human victor torments the vanquished, even when the latter is totally in his power. It is at this point that a third human peculiarity comes into operation.

We have already said that a cat cannot be supposed to identify with a mouse, and is therefore not being cruel to the mouse with which it plays, since it cannot imaginatively enter into the mouse's sufferings. Men, however, possess the capacity of identification as well as that of projection. They are able to enter into the pain of another, and to imagine what the sufferer feels. Upon this basis of identification with the insulted and injured rests man's charity and altruism: for no one would have been concerned to free slaves or to prevent child-labour unless, imaginatively, he could put himself into the shoes of a slave or an ill-treated child. But upon this basis also rests man's capacity for cruelty. His wish to torture and humiliate someone over whom he has already proved his superiority is clearly related to his ability to enter imaginatively into his enemy's agony.

There can be no doubt that we wish to behave to persecutors as we believe or fear that they would behave to us. There can be few people who, reading of Auschwitz or Belsen, have not had phantasies of submitting the torturers to the same punishments as they inflicted upon others. Humane, liberal people realize intellectually that such retaliation is useless. There is no point in adding to the sum of human barbarity by talion retribution. But even the most tender-hearted, often especially the most tender-hearted, generally react to the description of cruelty by feeling such hatred towards those who inflict it that their immediate emotional response is to wish them to suffer the same punishment.

It is because, in varying degree, we have all, as infants, had the experience of total helplessness combined with frustration and humiliation, that we can identify with the enemy we have rendered powerless, and wish him to experience still further pain and humiliation. The cruelty with which man treats his defeated enemy can only be understood in terms of retaliation and revenge. Scapegoats personify both power and weakness at the same time. We project the former attribute upon them and identify with the latter characteristic. Victor and vanquished thus become linked by a bond of mutual hatred which goes far beyond the aggressive struggle for dominance which we see in other animals; and our potential for cruelty is one price we pay for the singular prolongation of our dependency in childhood.

It will, no doubt, seem offensive and incredible to suggest that ordinary people have hidden paranoid tendencies and a proclivity for brutality. Yet the evidence is there. Public executions are still exciting spectacles to which mothers take their children in parts of the so-called civilized world; and it is not so long since, in our own country, traitors were dragged through the streets and publicly castrated before the executioner finally despatched them. It is a mistake to believe that the ordinary man is not capable of the extremes of cruelty. We may like to believe that the guards in the German concentration camps could be classified as abnormal, but many seem to have been ordinary men whose taste for cruelty had only to be reinforced by training and example for them to become accustomed to the daily, wanton infliction of abominable pain and humiliation. It is no use pretending that any of us are immune to sadistic feelings. Of course there are shining instances of human beings who, at the risk of their own lives, have refused to participate in barbarity – one has only to think of some of the doctors in concentration camps who refused to perform the horrible experimental operations demanded of them. But the catalogue of human cruelty is so long and the practice of torture so ubiquitous that it is impossible to believe that sadism is confined to a few abnormals. Indeed, any writer who dwells upon the details of man's cruelty to man is likely to be accused of merely seeking the widest public for his work rather than making a serious contribution to understanding, a fact which demonstrates the universality of public interest in the subject. We have to face the fact that man's proclivity for cruelty is rooted in his biological peculiarities, in common with his capacity for conceptual thought, for speech, and for creative achievement.

References

1. Gibbon, Edward, *The Decline and Fall of the Roman Empire* (London: Methuen, 1898), vol. VI, pp. 136–7.
2. Laski, Marghanita, 'The Hostile World', from *The World of Children* (London: Paul Hamlyn, 1966), p. 203.
3. Washburn, S. L., 'Conflict in Primate Society' in *Conflict in Society* (London: Ciba Foundation, J. & A. Churchill, 1966), p. 57.
4. Comfort, Alex, *Nature and Human Nature* (London: Weidenfeld & Nicolson, 1966; Harmondsworth: Penguin, p. 17).
5. Cohn, Norman, *Warrant for Genocide* (London: Eyre & Spottiswoode, 1967; Harmondsworth: Penguin).

Eleven

Psychopathic
Hostility

Depressive persons turn their hostility against themselves; schizoid persons withdraw from human contact in order to avoid the danger of expressing love or hate; paranoid persons deny their hostility still further, and attribute it to other people. In any of these groups of people, these methods of defence may occasionally fail, control be overwhelmed, and a violent act be committed which is out of character with the subject's normal personality.

In this chapter, we shall attempt to delineate a group of persons who combine certain paranoid characteristics with an habitual lack of ability to control their immediate impulses. These people, generally known as psychopaths, also carry with them into adult life more than the common endowment of hostility. They are, however, much more dangerous than depressives, schizoid personalities, or paranoid schizophrenics, since they have a strong propensity to 'act out' their hostility, and are therefore responsible for much violent crime.

The term 'psychopath' has, during the past few decades, been applied to so wide a variety of persons whose behaviour differs from the average that, as a diagnostic category, it is even more open to criticism than most psychiatric labels. Nevertheless, the term is sufficiently widely accepted for it to have been incorporated into English law (Mental Health Act, 1959), although many psychiatrists objected to this step at the time on the grounds that the concept implied lacked sufficient precision. We shall not here consider the creative personality, nor the sexual deviant, nor the chronically inadequate, although the word psychopath has been applied to all of these. We shall rather restrict our consideration to the so-called 'aggressive psychopath', a category which is fortunately more easily definable than any of the other abnormalities of personality subsumed under the general heading.

Recent research has revealed two facts about psychopathic people which indicate that, in some cases at any rate, organic, physical factors play a part, as well as psychopathology. Somewhere between a quarter and a half of aggressive psychopaths show abnormalities of the electrical rhythms of the brain, which can be detected and recorded by the electroencephalogram. A smaller proportion show genetic abnormalities. Examination of violent criminals in Rampton and Moss Side Hospitals has shown that just over two per cent have abnormalities of the sex chromosomes. There are several types of abnormality. One produces men who are unusually tall; another a physical type with some feminine characteristics. There is also some association of these genetic abnormalities with mental defect.

Much more research is needed to establish the varieties, physical and psychological, of psychopathic personalities. Many are of average or above average intelligence. The majority show no detectable physical abnormality. Although most psychopaths come from home backgrounds in which affection has been notably lacking, this association is not invariable. There can be no doubt, however, that there is a subsection of the population with less than average

control over immediate impulse; and that part of this subsection is suffering from defects of nature as well as of
nurture.

One of the most interesting facts to emerge from recent
criminological research is that crimes of violence, sexual
crimes, and dangerous driving offences are often committed
by the same type of person.[1] It is widely believed that
criminals commit only one type of offence. But a man who
commits a sexual offence is more likely, if he has any previous convictions, to have committed some crime other
than a sexual one. There is a chance of nearly one in three
that a motorist committing a serious driving offence will
already be known to the police as a suspected person or
have been previously convicted of a non-motoring offence.
Moreover, since about eighty per cent of persons serving
a first prison sentence never return to prison, it is obvious
that a high proportion of crime is committed by a small
number of people.

Aggressive psychopaths show, from their earliest years,
abnormal behaviour in relation both to people close to
them and also towards society as a whole. Perhaps the most
striking feature of this abnormality is a ruthless disregard
for the feelings of others. Egotistical, selfish and impulsive,
the aggressive psychopath tends to take what he wants at
the time irrespective of the needs or the rights of other
people. In doing so, he often shows an incredible lack of
foresight. The impulse of the moment is his master; and if
others obstruct the satisfaction of his immediate needs,
they may expect to suffer. In adult life, such a person often
becomes a criminal who does not hesitate to use violence if
it is necessary to gain his ends, and, when apprehended,
shows little remorse for conduct which would induce the
extreme of guilt in the majority of human beings.

In addition to violent behaviour, many psychopaths show

139

an almost total disregard for truth, and will tell any lie to gain their ends, or tell unnecessary and often foolish lies for no discernible reason. This tendency to lie is in part based upon a failure to form a relation with other people which would incur any obligation to tell the truth. It is also partly the result of an inability to distinguish truth from falsehood, and a tendency to take phantasy for fact.

Psychopathic abnormality is generally manifested from childhood onwards, but often escapes detection in the early years, since no one expects that a small child will be anything but egotistical. It is much to be hoped that methods of detecting young psychopaths will be developed; for a good deal of serious crime could thereby be prevented, and the child itself be given suitable treatment and care. Neville Heath, for example, who was hanged in 1946 for two sadistic murders, showed evidence of psychopathic abnormality from early childhood, although this did not emerge at his trial. At the age of eight he was caught severely thrashing a little girl and had to leave school as a result. He was also notoriously cruel to animals, a petty thief, a liar and unusually boastful. These character traits were well-established before puberty; and it is a sad reflection on our society that we do nothing about such people as Neville Heath before they have committed serious crimes.[2]

It is, of course, true that many children show disorders of behaviour of the kind described above without being psychopathic. But the majority of children do not exhibit all these traits together; and, if they behave anti-socially, do so only intermittently. Young psychopaths, moreover, show an absence of response to punishment; or, rather, they respond in a way which is the opposite of that which teachers and parents expect. The potential psychopath reacts to punishment with an increase of aggression rather than with a modification of his behaviour, and rapidly becomes regarded as incorrigible on this account.

Psychopaths are not insane, in the sense that they do not usually exhibit hallucinations, delusions, or other evidence of being grossly out of touch with reality. But they are inclined, to a far greater extent than is customary even among children, to confuse their own imaginations with reality. We have already mentioned the grandiose ideas with which paranoid schizophrenics attempt to preserve or salvage their tottering self-esteem. Psychopaths indulge in similar conceits and self-glorification, but, unlike the insane, are often successful in persuading others of the truth of their claims. Obtaining money by false pretences is a crime which is often committed by psychopaths, who assume false identities, tell extremely convincing, circumstantial stories about their past exploits and their present, temporary state of financial embarrassment, and thus impose upon the generous and deceive the gullible. One reason why psychopaths are so convincing is that they half believe their own stories. Uncertain of their actual identities, and held in far less esteem by their fellows than they would like, they invent fictitious personalities for themselves, embroider detail upon detail, and, like novelists who fall in love with their own fictions, come to believe that the invented character is at least as 'real' as the nonentity they see in the looking-glass. It is characteristic that Neville Heath should have been convicted in 1937 of 'posing as Lord Dudley', court-martialled in 1945 for wearing military decorations without authority, and fined in 1946 for wearing the uniform of a lieutenant-colonel, 'or sometimes of a major'. I remember interviewing a recidivist false pretender in prison, who was by then about seventy years old. It was impossible to tell how far he believed his own stories about himself. He had certainly been extremely successful in persuading other people to cash cheques for him and in convincing them that he was a well-known columnist on *The Daily Express*. Although not obviously insane, he had a number of paranoid ideas in which he almost certainly believed. In short, he was a man who demonstrated convincingly the inadequacy of our present psychiatric classifications, and the narrowness of the border-line between deliberate make-believe and psychotic delusion.

Psychopaths share with the schizophrenic the characteristic of living in a world which is predominantly solipsistic; that is, in which people and events are not valued in and for themselves, but only in so far as they affect the subject. It is certain that most psychopaths have not progressed emotionally to the stage of being able to experience depression. Their aggression and hatred remain directed outwards, and, when inhibited, are not turned inwards against the self. This fact accounts both for the absence of true depression, and for the lack of any sense of self-reproach or guilt. Like paranoid persons, they blame others rather than themselves; but, unlike the typical paranoid schizophrenic, they do not have the central conviction of being helpless against the attacks of much more powerful persecutors.

It is clear that it is fear which chiefly inhibits the expression of hostility in the other types of character we have examined, and fear which initiates the construction of elaborate psychopathological defences. Psychopaths remain alarmingly unafraid both of their own and of others' hostility. They commonly exhibit an unusual disregard for danger, whether this be a threat from other persons or else from situations upon which the average man looks with apprehension. Some of the most intrepid pilots of aircraft during the war were psychopaths whose abnormality secured them esteem in wartime, but whose ruthlessness and lack of inhibition made them intolerable to society in time of peace. Such men behave as if they were omnipotently immune from danger; and their courage is less impressive than it appears, since it is based upon a lack of appreciation of danger rather than upon a stalwart facing of real peril.

Psychopathic conduct can be explained, at any rate in part, by a failure to develop any affectional ties. As we have said, whatever part genetic or constitutional defects may play in contributing to this abnormality, there is no doubt that a high proportion of psychopaths come from homes where affection is lacking. More than is generally realized, the fact that most of us behave even relatively decently to our fellows is because we value their love and approval. We all start life as greedy and ruthless; but although, in extremity, when vital needs are threatened, we may revert to totally unscrupulous behaviour, we are ordinarily restrained both by the fear that we shall be disapproved of, and also by our capacity to identify ourselves with those whose interests conflict with our own.

It is certainly true that the fear of punishment exercises a deterrent effect upon the ordinary person who might be tempted to steal or to use violence upon someone who was obstructing him. But, as the history of our penal code convincingly demonstrates, there is little correlation between the severity of the punishment administered and its deterrent effect. It has always been difficult for penal reformers to persuade conventionally-minded people of this truth. Hence, when in 1814 Sir Samuel Romilly attempted to persuade Parliament that the penalty of hanging, drawing and quartering could safely be abolished, he failed to achieve his aim; for many members believed that there would be an immediate increase in the crimes of treason for which this barbarous method of execution was still the prescribed penalty. Similar fears were expressed when it

143

was first proposed to abolish hanging as a punishment for theft. Yet, so far as we understand human nature, the ordinary person will be deterred from crime by comparatively minor penalties, whilst the psychopath will not be deterred by any threat of punishment, however savage. Indeed, the more brutal punishments often provoke an increase of hatred and violence, rather than deterring the offender. In Chapter 5 we quoted a passage from the autobiography of a violent criminal, *The Courage of His Convictions*. Here is what he has to say about corporal punishment:

I should think the product I am today ought to prove thrashings are no good, and only produce responses of vengeance and violence. It makes me laugh when I read of the Tory women at Bournemouth calling for a return of the cat. Even on what you might call simply an economic basis, I and all the people I know would prefer the cat to a long sentence any time. After three days it doesn't hurt any more, and the scars soon heal except those on your mind. What you feel is anger, resentment, and, most of all, a determination somehow to get your own back. But being deterred? The idea never gets a look in.[3]

Quite apart from humanitarian considerations, there is little point in enacting savage penalties even for savage crime. For those comparatively normal people who are deterred from crime by the threat of punishment seem to be so, not because the penalty itself is so unpleasant, but because the fact of being punished implies the disapproval of society and a loss of status for the individual. This is easily seen in children, who, if they are dependent upon the love and approval of their parents, are distressed by even a mild punishment, since this implies a withdrawal of the affectionate approval which they value. In other words, the effect of punishment cannot be regarded as a simple response to a noxious stimulus but can only be understood if the circumstances and personal relationship of both the

144

punished and the punisher are taken into account. Psychopathic people fail to respond to, or to be deterred by, punishment, partly because they are impulsive and lack foresight, but chiefly because they have failed to develop any ordinary bonds of affection with their fellows. Like the Miller of Dee, the psychopath announces by his conduct 'I care for nobody, no, not I, since nobody cares for me.' Since he does not believe that anyone really values him, he has little to lose by anti-social conduct, nor any motive for telling the truth. Deprivation of society's approval means nothing to a man who has never felt that it was accorded him.

Moreover, the psychopath's failure to develop the capacity for identification with others, which is a correlate of affectionate dependence, means that he has a strong tendency to regard other human beings as things rather than as persons. For him, other people seem either to be obstacles in the way of his desires, or else means by which he can obtain gratification. There is little concept of personal relationship, no valuing of another person as a being like himself with whom he can form a relationship on equal terms.

Thus, psychopaths are capable of treating other people as most of us might treat a wasp. The violence which they inflict upon others is often more like that of an unthinking child than the revengeful retaliation which we discussed in the last chapter, and which, we concluded, depended partly upon the capacity for identification with the victim. Psychopaths, therefore, do not pick on particular individuals or groups as a focus for their hostility in the way in which paranoid schizophrenics do, but since they are full of resentment against everyone, it is easy to teach them to enjoy the exercise of cruelty. It is probable that some of the sadistic guards in the concentration camps were psychopaths who readily accepted the idea that Jews were less than human, and welcomed the opportunity of behaving sadistically in much the same way as a child could be taught to enjoy tormenting animals.

The problem of detecting and dealing effectively with psychopathic people is one which society has hardly begun to tackle. Judging from the accounts available of Scandinavian penal institutions, it is possible to reform some psychopathic criminals provided enough time is available. Cynics will allege that many psychopaths improve with time in any case, which is certainly true in some instances. But it also seems probable that treatment directed towards integrating the psychopath into a community rather than attempting to probe his individual psychology has sometimes had the effect of enabling him to form links with other human beings which were previously absent, and thus of modifying his anti-social behaviour.

References

1. Willett, T. C., *Criminal on the Road* (London: Tavistock, 1964).
2. Playfair, Giles, and Sington, Derrick, *The Offenders* (London: Secker & Warburg, 1957), p. 43.
3. Parker, Tony, and Allerton, Robert, *The Courage of his Convictions* (London: Hutchinson, 1962), p. 34.

Twelve

Ways of
Reducing
Hostility

Psychiatrists, because they are used to taking responsibility
for other people's emotional problems, and because their
training has encouraged them to believe that they have a
special insight into human nature, are apt to proffer advice
in fields of human activity where they are no more than in-
experienced amateurs. This is especially true in the spheres
of social administration and politics, in which, although the
human factor may ultimately be decisive, day-to-day decisions have to be taken on a pragmatic basis which largely
neglects the emotional aspects of human nature with which
psychiatrists are chiefly concerned. It would be Utopian to
think, therefore, that insights derived from ethology,
psycho-analysis, or allied disciplines are likely to have any
immediate effect upon the conduct of politicians or the
course of world events. We and our children, overshadowed
as we are by the threat of nuclear catastrophe, must count
ourselves fortunate to survive from year to year: and we
must not expect that, in our lifetimes, the conduct of human
affairs is likely to alter for the better in any obvious way.

Nevertheless, in the long term, the way in which we regard human nature, and the increasing knowledge which
we can undoubtedly gain about ourselves, is bound to have
its effect. It would be as foolish to neglect the psychological

147

and biological view of man as it would be to believe that the acceptance of this point of view will bring about an immediate improvement in our human lot. This chapter, therefore, is concerned with the application of our very limited knowledge of human psychology to the problem of controlling hostility, in the hope that, eventually, our descendants will find themselves less menaced than we are by the threat of total destruction.

Control of the destructive aspects of hostility between human beings can be approached from two different, yet complementary angles. One is to consider in what way it is possible to reduce the paranoid element in hostility, that is, to prevent aggression from turning into hate. The other is to see how to encourage the expression of the more positive aspects of the aggressive drive. In the latter connection it is pertinent to recall Dr Winnicott's remark, already quoted in Chapter 5, to the effect that, 'If society is in danger, it is not because of man's aggressiveness, but because of the repression of personal aggressiveness in individuals.'

Throughout this book, I have endeavoured to make it plain that aggression is a drive as innate, as natural, and as powerful as sex, and that the theory that aggression is nothing but a response to frustration is no longer tenable in the light of biological research. It is vitally important that we finally discard the kind of futile optimism which is implicit in the frustration-aggression hypothesis, and face the fact that, in man, as in other animals, the aggressive drive is an inherited constant, of which we cannot rid ourselves, and which is absolutely necessary for survival.

Psychiatrists, and especially psycho-analysts, are often expected to give advice upon the proper way in which children should be reared, and have not been reluctant to assume this responsibility. Yet, as Charles Rycroft, himself a psycho-analyst, recently pointed out in *Psycho-Analysis*

Observed,[1] there is no reason to assume that psycho-
analysts are better equipped to advise parents in this respect
than other human beings. The analyst's main task is to
understand his patient, and to help his patient to understand himself; and he moves out of his proper sphere when
he professes to be an expert in methods of education and
child care. Nevertheless, there is little doubt that increasing
knowledge and understanding of the needs of small children will in time lead to more concern about meeting these
needs, and will therefore lead to some diminution of the
hostility which, in adult life, derives from childhood deprivation. Professor Washburn's remark about the casual
way in which infants are treated is very much to the point.
We know that the emotional climate of the earliest years
and the way in which infants are handled is of vital importance for their future development as happy and healthy
human beings. Yet, although vague exhortations to love
our children better are constantly proffered, the amount
of hard fact about the effects of deprivation and mishandl-
ing is regrettably small, and evidence on which to give positive advice about child-rearing is minimal.

Should babies be swaddled or left free, and what is the
result upon character in later life of these alternative
methods? How much should a mother devote herself to the
care of her infant, and how much is it safe, or even desir-
able, that she should share the burden of infant care with
other members of the household? Are children likely to
develop more equably in a family in which there are grand-
parents, aunts, and cousins under the same roof; or is the
concentration of loving care which they may obtain from
a devoted couple with neither the interference nor the support of other relatives more likely to promote their emotional equilibrium? Is the prolongation of breast-feeding
beyond the period fashionable in Western culture harmful

or of positive benefit? To all these, and many similar questions, we do not know the answers. Yet the direct observation of small infants by research workers like René Spitz,[2] who are concerned with the earliest stages of emotional development, will, in time, provide some of the answers: and, already, ethological studies in other species are producing information which we did not have before. The Harlows' work with infant monkeys has already been quoted in earlier chapters. One surprising and reassuring conclusion from their studies is that the effects of maternal deprivation can be greatly obviated if the deprived infant is provided with sufficient companionship of its own age. Although our information is at present grossly deficient, it is not unreasonable to hope that, in time, human mothers will be able to supplement their instinctive wisdom with a generally accepted body of knowledge about how best to meet their children's needs, and that the result of this will be a diminution of the number of individuals in the world whose aggression has been converted into hatred.

It is arguable that, under the conditions of modern civilization, the aggressive component in man is no longer biologically adaptive in the way that it was when men were nomadic hunters. But the speed of biological change is slow. No mutation has occurred to render us radically different from our prehistoric ancestors: and we possess the same instinctive equipment which served to ensure the survival of men for whom existence was a perpetual struggle. In earlier chapters, we have linked man's peculiar aggressiveness with his dependency; and we have also pointed out that paranoid people think of themselves as weak and their imagined persecutors as strong. Part of the human proclivity for paranoid beliefs may be phylogenetic rather than ontogenetic. For man, as a species, is singularly ill-equipped with natural means of defence or attack. His skin is thin and sensitive compared with the hides of many mammals, and he lacks even sufficient hair to keep himself warm. He has no horns, his nails are not strong enough to use as claws, and his teeth, though well adapted for mastication, are too small to be effective as weapons. No wonder men are prone to regard themselves as weak and ill-protected. In terms of comparative zoology, they are both.

Because of the development of his brain, man has been able to compensate for his natural lack of aggressive and defensive equipment by the invention of weapons. Indeed, it is probable that the invention of weapons preceded the evolution of *homo sapiens*, and that the reduction in size of the formidable canine teeth which characterized our ape-like progenitors occurred because these natural weapons had been supplanted by artificial ones. It is likely that Australopithecus, a species intermediate between anthropoid apes and man, with a brain only a little larger than that of a gorilla, used primitive weapons in hunting.[3] Man, the unspecialized and unprotected primate, has had to be clever to survive: but his cleverness has overreached itself. The invention of primitive weapons was necessary; and, if it had not taken place, *homo sapiens* might never have persisted or even evolved. But modern weapons are far from being direct substitutes for teeth or claws; and, although the cynic might call the hydrogen bomb adaptive, in that it may solve the problem of over-population, he can hardly maintain that nuclear weapons promote the survival of man in the same manner as a spear or a hand axe did when these weapons were first invented.

The development of weapons is of considerable psychological interest, since there is a vast difference emotionally between slaughtering an enemy at a distance, and attempting to kill him at close quarters. If human fights were confined to fisticuffs, an appreciable number of human beings

151

would still be killed; for, as we have seen, man's paranoid potential overrides the operation of the natural inhibitions which prevent most animals from dispatching their defeated opponents. Moreover, as Konrad Lorenz has pointed out, it is just because human beings are so ill-equipped with natural weapons that they lack strong inhibitions against injuring their own species. Better-armed animals are better protected by inhibitions against intra-specific aggression; and if men had tusks or horns they would be less, rather than more, likely to kill one another. The artificial weapon is too cerebral a device for nature to have provided adequate safeguards against it. Nevertheless, traces of inhibiting mechanisms do remain in that many humans recoil at kicking an enemy when he is down, or will even feel pity for, and extend help to, a wounded opponent. All traces of this 'decent' behaviour disappear, however, as soon as a moderate distance is interposed between contestants. It is obviously true that most bomber pilots are no better and no worse than other men. The majority of them, given a can of petrol and told to pour it over a child of three and ignite it, would probably disobey the order. Yet, put a decent man in an aeroplane a few hundred feet above a village, and he will, without compunction, drop high explosives and napalm and inflict appalling pain and injury on men, women and children. The distance between him and the people he is bombing makes them into an impersonal target, no longer human beings like himself with whom he can identify.

Although the theoretical strategists of nuclear warfare cannot be accused of injuring other human beings in the way that a bomber pilot can, the terms in which they discuss the 'unthinkable' show the operation of the same kind of mechanism. 'Distance' from other people need not be physical; it may simply be psychological. As Anatol Rapoport has pointed out in his *Strategy and Conscience*,[4] the human faculty of abstraction removes the content of a problem and enables the strategist to discuss nuclear threats and counter-threats as if human beings were not involved at all. The new word 'megadeath' may be useful in abstract strategic discussion; translated into the actual experience of Hiroshima and Nagasaki it becomes an obscenity.

Distance, physical or psychological, makes abstraction possible. Man's cleverness can put a distance between himself and natural feeling, based on instinct, which makes all kinds of horrors conceivable. It is obviously impractical to suggest that the walls of the Pentagon and of the Kremlin should be covered with photographs of Hiroshima in order to remind strategists of the reality underlying their discussions. Yet a recent President of the United States found it necessary to have a reminder on his desk that 'The buck stops here' as if he could not quite believe in the reality of his own ultimate responsibility. It would be no bad thing if military strategists should compel themselves to contemplate some reminder of that with which they are really concerned.

The invention of weapons which kill at a great distance combined with man's capacity for abstraction, is one great threat to human survival. Theoretically, therefore, the abolition of weapons, especially of nuclear weapons, is an obvious step towards preserving the continuity of our species. Is disarmament a practical possibility?

Reluctantly, I am compelled to admit that I see no prospect of it. The need for weapons is rooted in man's biological weakness and vulnerability; and the fact that modern weapons have become absurdly and indiscriminately destructive does not, unfortunately, make it more likely that we can entirely rid ourselves of them. In a thoughtful and excellent book, *The Control of the Arms*

Race, Hedley Bull argues that the achievement of peaceful stability is more likely to be brought about by intelligent agreements between the nuclear powers than by attempts to get rid of these dreadful weapons. One of the most hopeful features of the international situation at the time of writing is that America and Russia appear to be seeking just the kind of intelligent agreement which Mr Bull advocates, in that each government is concerned to limit expenditure on enormously costly systems of defence against the missiles of the other side, whilst preserving the 'balance of terror' as it now exists.

I also agree with Mr Bull in his assumption that, in the foreseeable future, we have to accept that we shall continue to live in a world of sovereign states which are potentially hostile to one another. As he says,

> ... The world of sovereign states which are armed and divided is a dangerous one, in which there is no absolute security from war and defeat.... We cannot expect that the establishment of a universal government by contract among the nations rather than by conquest will be brought about by governments incapable of the most modest forms of cooperation: that the complete and voluntary elimination of national armaments will be put into effect by governments, for all of whom there are issues over which they will resort to violence rather than accept defeat: or that the removal of the sources of political conflicts (by psychological treatment, education, moral regeneration or political indoctrination) will be undertaken by governments themselves absorbed in such conflicts.[5]

The vision of a universal government with the monopoly of nuclear power is enticing, however remote it may seem. In our present state of knowledge, however, I think it must be regarded as a Utopian concept as unlikely of fulfilment as Melanie Klein's hope that child analysis will become part of every person's upbringing. Man is a competitive, aggressive, territorial animal. He is also a social animal who needs both the support of others of his own kind and opponents from whom he can distinguish himself in order to affirm his own sense of identity. Given these biological and psychological characteristics, it seems as unlikely that the sovereign state will be abolished as that all baboons should band together in one troop instead of living together in separate communities as they do at present. We have considered, in an earlier chapter, the conflicts which spring up, inevitably, in groups of men who are closely identified with one another. It is inconceivable that the whole of mankind should unite under one government unless the Earth were threatened by destruction from another planet or by some cosmic catastrophe. Indeed, it is arguable that we should not be attempting to bring men together into yet larger aggregations under one government, but rather attempting to split them up into smaller groups with greater autonomy.

One feature of modern existence which tends to convert aggression into hate is the size and complexity of civilized institutions. When a man is, or feels himself to be, an unimportant cog in a very large machine, he is deprived of the chance of aggressive self-affirmation, and of a proper pride and dignity. His sense of ineffectiveness is bound to re-awaken the earliest feelings of helplessness and weakness which he had as a child, with a corresponding tendency for his unexpressed, normal aggression to turn into hate and resentment. The self-employed craftsman with a sense of achievement is less likely to be hostile to his fellows than the organization man who feels himself to be nobody.

Very large aggregations of human beings are inimical to a sense of personal value, as is the concentration of power in one place. I believe that men are more likely to be happy when they live in relatively small communities in which they feel they have a personal stake and sufficient access to

155

power to believe that they exert some influence in determining the conditions of their own lives. Even in so small a country as Britain, there is a feeling amongst communities remote from London that their needs are not understood and therefore neglected: hence the periodic resurgence of national sentiment in Scotland and Wales, and the disaffection of southern Ireland. It is difficult, even in Great Britain, for all the citizens to feel themselves part of the main.

There is some evidence to suggest that productivity drops with collectivization. According to one recent writer, privately owned plots of land account for only three per cent of the total area under cultivation in Soviet Russia. Yet this minute proportion produces almost half the vegetables, meat and milk, three quarters of the eggs, and two thirds of the potatoes which Russia consumes.[6] Ideally, men should live in communities which are sufficiently small for them to maintain their identities and to encourage individual productivity, and which are in perpetual rivalry with other neighbouring small communities. Jung once made the comment that Swiss internal politics were the bitterest in his experience; yet Switzerland has succeeded in avoiding war at times when most other European nations have become embroiled in it. No doubt it is Switzerland's peculiar geography which is partially responsible for the avoidance of external conflict. It may also be that rivalry between canton and canton has helped to internalize the aggression of the Swiss as Jung suggests.

It is extremely unfortunate that the complexities of Western civilization tend to produce collective man rather than individuals. The mergers between aircraft firms, motor manufacturers and other producers of Western technical products are unhealthy psychologically, because, on the one hand, the enormous size of the companies reduces the opportunities available for men to realize their separate identities, and, on the other, they diminish the possibility of rivalry which exists when a small number of firms are making similar, but not identical, products. In wartime, men may be able to identify themselves with the whole country. In peace, it is easier for them to identify with a village, a county, or a canton. Moreover, it is much more difficult to project images of malignant aggressors upon one's near neighbour than it is upon a remote country whose inhabitants one does not know and whose language one does not speak.

It is, of course, possible to suggest ways of reducing the likelihood of paranoid projection between nations and groups. Most of these ways are already well known to human beings, though they are not pursued by governments with the vigour one would wish. The gross inequality which at present exists between nation and nation is an obvious breeding ground of hostility; and, over the long term, the industrialization of backward countries and the more equitable distribution of wealth will reduce envy and hatred.

Mutual agreement between governments as to what languages should be taught in schools is another possibility. The tendency to assume hostility in others is reduced by the possibility of communication; and, if English, French or Russian were universally spoken, some sources of misunderstanding would be eliminated. I well remember seeing a distinguished scientist whose underlying paranoid personality structure only emerged when he travelled abroad. Directly he crossed the Channel he became convinced that the populace were hostile to him, and assumed that everyone was making derogatory remarks about him because he could not understand what was being said. On his return to this country his symptoms largely disappeared.

157

It is obvious that the encouragement of the international exchange of students and the promotion of intermarriage between dissimilar populations can do nothing but good. More important still is the deliberate reduction of hostile propaganda between nations who have developed different political systems.

In *Fights, Games and Debates* Anatol Rapoport[7] has discussed the application of game theory to international disputes. In playing a game, one usually assumes that one's opponent is a human being like oneself who will make much the same choices as oneself in the dilemmas with which a game faces him. In conflicts of interest between nations, however, this natural assumption is often replaced by the attribution to the opponent of totally unrealistic hostility.

The wild generalizations which 'capitalists' make about 'communists' are only matched in absurdity by the generalizations which 'communists' make about 'capitalists' or indeed about heretical deviationists from their own brand of political philosophy. Rapoport, in a brilliant close to his book, makes a communist defend the capitalist case and a capitalist propound the communist thesis of society, and shows that if only opponents can be persuaded to make the 'assumption of similarity' in each other which they would normally do in a game of skill, the projections upon each other which are at the root of irrational hostility will largely disappear.

We urgently need international studies to determine what political and psychological factors have enabled certain countries to avoid war in spite of man's proclivity for engaging in it. Meanwhile, it is obvious that the encouragement of competition in all possible fields is likely to diminish the kind of hostility which leads to war rather than to increase it. At a conference of the Institute of Biology in 1963, I suggested that, far from deploring expenditure on the space race, we ought to welcome it.[8] For this kind of competition can be regarded as a ritualization of conflict equivalent to the ritual conflicts of animals which diminish the likelihood of war rather than encourage it. In the same way, rivalry between nations in sport can do nothing but good; and it should be possible to encourage competition in other fields also. Is it fantastic to suggest that the United Nations or some other international organization might set aside part of its funds to institute a series of yearly international competitions? There is no reason that I can see why nations of roughly equal status should not compete every year to see which could produce the most efficient mental hospital, the safest car, the best designed council house, and so on through an endless range of possibilities. This is merely an extension of the scheme of Nobel prizes; and it would not be difficult to engender intense national enthusiasm about products which affect everyone in our culture in the same way as it is easy to arouse enthusiasm about football with such devices as the World Cup.

Konrad Lorenz, in his book *On Aggression*,[9] has discussed the biological function of sport as a ritualized, competitive struggle between members of the human species which does not result in slaughter. He is supported in his views by Professor Wynne-Edwards, whose work upon territoriality has already been cited. In *Animal Dispersion* the latter writes:

Direct competition between individuals, therefore, has generally come to assume conventional forms, and the individuals are adapted or conditioned to accept as final in the great majority of cases decisions reached by clearly symbolic methods. Brute force and mutual savagery among members of the same species has at most a residual place in social competition.[10]

If this were as true of human society as it is of most animal societies, we should not need to fear the hydrogen bomb. As things stand at present, however, there are a number of factors which militate against the human species behaving as sensibly as their animal cousins.

In the course of this chapter, we have already discussed some of these, in which man's potential for paranoid projection is one, the invention of artificial weapons another, and the aggregation of mankind into large societies in which individuality is submerged a third. A fourth factor which encourages the expression of man's aggression in the form of destructive hostility, and which operates against the ritualization of aggression in the form of conventional competition, is man's appalling increase in numbers. Overpopulation is, paradoxically, the greatest threat to man's continuance as a species.

In an earlier chapter, it was pointed out that, in man as in other species, overcrowding is an undoubted breeding ground of hostility. We all need space in which to operate; although how large this space ought to be for each human being, or for each family, is a matter to which little thought has yet been accorded. It is now an urgent problem, on account of the population explosion which, immediately, threatens us all. It may well be that, before the end of the century, men will be attacking and destroying each other for the simple reason that there is not enough food to go round. Although agricultural experts have asserted that modern methods of food production could so increase the world's food supply that this planet could support a population of 45,000 million, there is no sign as yet that the supply of food is capable of keeping pace with the population. Indeed, in 1965, world population increased by two per cent, whilst food production only increased by one per cent. Already, starvation is threatening millions throughout the developing countries; but population is increasing at so accelerated a pace that, by the year 2000, there will be twice as many human beings on this earth as there are today.

Even if the problem of food supply could be surmounted, this increase in numbers of human beings must result in a corresponding increase of hostility; unless the under-populated areas of the world could be made inhabitable. As Western civilization spreads, so will urbanization and the consequent collection of human beings into large aggregate clusters, living closely packed together. We have come a long way from the days when primitive man roamed the earth in small groups of fifty to sixty. The self-limiting checks which, in animal populations, prevent both over-crowding and overpopulation were operative in primitive man, or else his numbers would have increased earlier. Modern civilizations have discarded infanticide and discouraged abortion. Some primitive societies forbid sexual intercourse with a lactating woman, and reduce feminine fertility by encouraging mothers to breast-feed their children for three years or longer. Modern societies do neither; and, because they are affluent, make early marriage possible for an increasing number of people. The great pandemics which used to reduce population have largely been abolished. It is estimated that the Black Death, which ravaged Europe in the fourteenth century, killed seventy-five million persons. Now it is famine, rather than disease, which decimates societies. Modern medicine and hygiene have so decreased the death rate that, every day, twice as many people are born as die. The psychological problems with which this book has been chiefly concerned pale into insignificance before the dreadful fact that, every year, the world has sixty-three million new mouths to feed.

The population explosion is, of all possible factors, the

most likely to cause an explosion of a different variety. The hydrogen bomb is undoubtedly the most effective way of reducing world population: and the most fearful expression of hostility yet devised. Who can doubt that, the more of us there are, the more likely we are to be destroyed by the ultimate explosion?

It follows from this argument that to reduce world population, or at least to stem the flood of its increase, is the most important single step which can be taken by mankind to reduce hostile tension. Every other consideration ought to be subsidiary to this, even perhaps our natural impulse to extend charity, and medical and financial aid to undeveloped countries. This sounds, and is, a cruel statement. But, wherever hygiene is taught, diet improved, and medical care made available, the result is a rapid decrease in the death rate, especially in infant mortality, combined with an increase in the birth rate. The result is that, within a short space of time there are far more mouths to feed, and the eventual sum of human misery is increased by the very methods which were originally designed to relieve it.

Humanitarian considerations will preclude us from preventing the spread of Western medicine. We cannot refuse to cure disease, nor to feed the starving. But we must insist that control of the birth rate goes hand-in-hand with social amelioration. The price of a higher standard of living is family limitation. Control of death must be accompanied by control of birth or we are doomed. Indeed, it may already be too late. For, in countries where Roman Catholicism is the prevailing religion, and where modern medicine is beginning to appear, the population will double in as little as twenty-three years.

If all countries were as efficient as Japan, which has halved her birth rate in the last twenty years, the problem could probably be solved in a rational way. Tragically, it seems more likely that the hydrogen bomb will provide the final solution.

The fact that, within the lifetimes of even the middle-aged, the world is going to face an inescapable increase in hostile tension, puts an increasing burden on political leaders. In an earlier chapter something was said of the danger of entrusting a country's welfare to the hands of visionaries or paranoiacs. The example of Hitler is too recent to be forgotten; but any country in which a large proportion of the population is in despair might throw up another leader of similar type. Moreover, even countries such as our own have not solved the problem of getting rid of leaders who become senile or mentally ill. One of the most disastrous political decisions of recent years was made by a prime minister who was under such tension that he was taking amphetamine, a drug which notoriously impairs judgement. It should be possible to devise a political system by which a leader who is judged to be unfit by his colleagues could be made to retire without his immediate rivals being accused of ambitious self-seeking. Politicians are generally men of high intelligence as well as possessing more than their common share of the aggressive drive. Nevertheless, the fact that they are in the first place self-selected, and that, unlike other professions, they are not required to give evidence of either knowledge or wisdom by submitting to courses of study or to examinations, means that they are subject to fewer checks on their suitability for their chosen profession than doctors or lawyers. It should not be impossible to improve our selection of those who rule us.

As a practical system for controlling and making use of the competitive aggression which is so evident in political controversy, democracy seems the best system yet devised. Although slow and uncertain in operation, democracy has the decided advantage over other political systems of providing an opposition which not only acts as a check on government, but also gives scope for passionate disagreement. Indeed, the House of Commons might stand as an exemplar of how men should deal with their aggressive drives: for it provides 'enemies' who are clearly serving a useful function; it encourages the expression of opposite opinion; yet, by bringing opponents face to face as human beings, it makes it difficult for them to project paranoid images upon each other. Indeed, it has often been remarked that political opponents, in countries where free speech is allowed, may be privately friendly though bitterly antagonistic in public. Although it is probable that Western states are premature in their attempts to foist democracy upon countries who are not ready for it, and which may well be temporarily better served by the communist system, it is hard to fault democracy as an ideal psychologically.

In conclusion, I would like to make a plea for further research. We are threatened as a species by our own destructiveness, and we shall never learn to control this unless we understand ourselves better. Throughout history, man has been bedevilled by ignorance about his own nature, and has filled the gap by Utopian phantasies of what he wishes to be like rather than face the reality of what he is. As this book has amply demonstrated, our lack of knowledge is still appalling. There is so much that we do not know, so much that we could find out. If man is to survive, we need to know all that we possibly can about ourselves, our development, our needs, our institutions, our advantages and our failings. Man, though successful biologically, is in many ways an unsatisfactory species; but, whatever he is, we have to live with him.

References

1. Rycroft, Charles, *Psycho-Analysis Observed* (London: Constable, 1966; Harmondsworth: Penguin).
2. Gaskill, Herbert S. (ed.), *Counterpoint*, A Tribute to René A. Spitz (New York: International Universities Press, 1963).
3. Le Gros Clark, Sir Wilfred E., *Man-Apes or Ape-Men* (New York: Holt, Rinehart & Winston, 1967).
4. Rapoport, Anatol, *Strategy and Conscience* (New York: Harper & Row, 1964).
5. Bull, Hedley, *The Control of the Arms Race* (London: Weidenfeld & Nicolson, 1961), pp. 202–3.
6. Ardrey, Robert, *The Territorial Imperative* (London: Collins, 1967), pp. 115–16.
7. Rapoport, Anatol, *Fights, Games and Debates* (Ann Arbor, Mich.: University of Michigan Press, 1960).
8. Storr, Anthony, 'Possible Substitutes for War', in Carthy and Ebling (eds.), *The Natural History of Aggression* (London: Academic Press, 1964), p. 143.
9. Lorenz, Konrad, *On Aggression* (London: Methuen, 1966).
10. Wynne-Edwards, V. C., *Animal Dispersion in Relation to Social Behaviour* (Edinburgh: Oliver & Boyd, 1962), p. 131.

Further Reading

Berkowitz, Leonard, *Aggression: Social Psychological Analysis* (New York: McGraw-Hill, 1962).

Ciba Foundation, *Conflict in Society* (London: J. & A. Churchill, 1966).

Carthy, J. D., and Ebling, F. J. (eds.), *The Natural History of Aggression* (London: Academic Press, 1964).

Frank, Jerome D., *Sanity and Survival* (London: Barrie & Rockliff, The Cresset Press, 1967).

Fromm, Erich, *The Anatomy of Human Destructiveness* (New York: Holt, Rinehart & Winston, 1973).

Gardiner, Muriel, *The Deadly Innocents* (London: Hogarth Press, 1977).

Gurr, Ted R., and Graham, Hugh D., *The History of Violence in America* (New York: Bantam Books, 1969).

Lorenz, Konrad, *On Aggression* (London: Methuen, 1966).

Renvoize, Jean, *Web of Violence* (London: Routledge & Kegan Paul, 1978).

Rochlin, Gregory, *Man's Aggression* (Boston: Gambit, 1973).

Russell, Claire, and Russell, W. M. S., *Violence, Monkeys and Man* (London: Macmillan, 1968).

Wynne-Edwards, V. C., *Animal Dispersion in Relation to Social Behaviour* (Edinburgh: Oliver & Boyd, 1962).

Yates, Aubrey J., *Frustration and Conflict* (London: Methuen, 1962).

Index

abstraction, faculty of, 153
Adler, Alfred, 19–20, 74–5, 81
adrenal glands, the, 29
anger, effects of, 27–30, 34, 36, 126
animals, 34, *see also* names of species
  anger in, 28–9
  experiments with, 32–3
  fighting among, 40–45, 52, 55, 124–5
  over-population of, 52–3
  polygamous, 43
  predatory, 40–42, 124, 133
  societies of, 42–3, 57
  territorial, 52–3
anxiety-hysteria, 19
appeasement gestures, 55–7, 125
Aristotle, 77
armies, 46
Australopithecus, 151

baboons, 42, 44, 155
Barnett, S. A., 27
Basil II, Emperor, 125
Beethoven, Ludwig van, 122
behaviour, types of, 27, 33

beliefs, 79–81
bereavement, 104–7
Berkowitz, Leonard, 35
bird-song, 52–3
bond-behaviour, 56–7
brain, the, 28–30, 32, 151
Bull, Hedley, 154
Bergson, 19

Cannon, W. B., 28
caste systems and outcasts, 43–4, 132–3
child-analysis, 16–17, 75
children, *see also* infants
  development of, 10, 64–73, 79, 82, 93, 116, 129
  fears of, 62
  mothers and, *see* mothers
  phantasies of, 70–73
  rearing of, 67–70, 87–8, 98, 112, 148–50; ideal, 37, 98
  sex differences, 86
Christian Church, the, 80
Christianity, 90, 107, 110
Churchill, Sir Winston, 47
cichlid fish, 34, 56, 89
Cohn, Norman, 76, 132

Index

collectivization, 156–7
competition, 51, 83
  international, 158–60
  among animals:
    for females, 42–3
    for food, 40–42
    for territory, 52, 56
concentration camps, 10, 133, 134, 135, 145
Courage of his Convictions, The, 71, 87, 144
creative achievements, 78, 89, 97, 121
criminals, 138–40
  deterrence of, 143–4
  reform of, 146
cruelty, 124–9, 132–5
  psychopathic, 140, 145–6
  sadism, 18, 91
cultural differences, 88

danger, group effects of, 47–9
Darwin, Charles, 42
de Gaulle, General Charles, 120
De Vore, Irven, 44
de Vos, George, 43
deaf, the, 122
death, loss by, 105–7
death instinct, the, 15, 20–25
democracy, 45–7, 163–4
dependency on others, 66–8, 74, 81, 99, 109–12
  of infants, 66–8, 111, 112, 116–18, 129, 134
depression, 102–12, 114, 131, 137, 142
disarmament, nuclear, 153
distance, 83
  required between animals, 52–4, 55, 57, *see also* overcrowding

effect on warfare, 151–3
dominance:
  hierarchies of, 43–4, 46–7
  illusions of, 116
  will for, 11, 19, 37

Eddington, A. S., 83
education, power of, 78
Eibl-Eibesfeldt, Irenaus, 32
electrical stimulation, 32–3
emotion, effects of, 28, *see also* anger
enemies, 83, 106–7

fairy tales, 62, 70–72
fathers, 72–3, *see also* parents
fear, 142–3
female aggression, 85–8, 92, 94–6
fighting, among animals, 40–45, 52, 55, 124–5
  among men, *see* war
food, competition for, 40–42
Freud, Sigmund, 15, 18–23, 39, 81, 111, 119
frustration, 64, 127

geese, 56, 104
Gibbon, Edward, 11, 12, 125
gibbons, 85
Gibson, Eleanor, 64
government, *see* leadership
  universal, 154

Hall, K. R. L., 44
Hamburger, Michael, 122
Harlow, H. F. and M. K., 66, 69, 109, 150
hatred, 96, 99, 126
Heath, Neville, 140–41
Heiligenberg, Walter, 35
heretics, 80, 82

hippopotamus, the, 53
hostility, control of, 148–64
House of Commons, the, 83, 164
Humperdinck, E., 63
Huxley, Aldous, 77
hypothalamus, the, 29–30

identification, self-, 49, 80–83, 110
  in suffering, 133
identity, human, 79, 82–3, 97, 106–7
infants, 128, 150, *see also* children
  dependency of, 66–7, 111, 112, 116–17, 128, 134
  development of, *see under* children
  frustration in, 63
  mother, relation to, 25, 66, 106, 108–9, 111–12, 117
  phantasies of, 16, 24, 60–61, 63, 67
  pleasure of, 21–2
insecurity, emotional, 90–91, 95–6, 99
instinctive behaviour, 22, 27, 31
intellectual activity, 10–11, 88, 115, 121
international goodwill, 157–9
intolerance, 132
Isaiah, 75

Japan, 132, 162
Jews, 132
Jones, Ernest, 19
Jung, Carl Gustav, 81, 94, 156

Kinsey, Alfred C., 34
Klein, Melanie, 17, 23–5, 60–61, 63, 75, 154

Kuo, Zing Yang, 32, 33
Kurelu people, New Guinea, 57–8

language, 10–11, 37
languages, 157
leadership, 45–8
  illness of leaders, 120–21, 163
Lorenz, Konrad, 34, 41, 55, 56, 57, 152, 159
love, and aggression, 57, 90, 96, 107
  defence against, 114–23
  need for, 96–100, 107–10, 114

male aggression, 17–18, 85, 86–8, 91–3
male neurosis, 96
marriage, 94–7, *see also* sexual relationship
Matthews, Harrison, 55
Matthiessen, Peter, 59
Maugham, W. Somerset, 106–7
memory, 24, 128
monkeys, infant, 66, 69; *see also* species
Morris, T. and Blom-Cooper, L., 96
mothers:
  animal, 85
  and children, 25, 61–3, 66–7, 72–3, 82, 108–9, 111–12, 117, 149–50
  death of, 105–6
murder, 96–7, 111, 112, 131
  inhibitions against, 152
music, 78, 88–9, 122
mythology, 61–3, 70–73, 75–7

N.S.P.C.C., 125
national sentiment, 156–9

under-developed nations, 157, 162
natural selection, 40, 41–3
Nazi Germany, 132, *see also* concentration camps
neurosis, 61
  neurotic people, 94–6
nuclear disarmament, 153
nuclear weapons, *see under* weapons

overcrowding, effects of, 53–5, 159–60
over-population, *see* population explosion

paranoid schizophrenia, 130–33, 137, 142
parents, 67–71, 72–3, 105–6, 127, *see also* mothers
Peckham Health Centre, 65
pecking-order, 43
persecution:
  imagined, 130–33
  of the weak, 125–6
phantasy:
  archetypal, 61–2, 72–3, 76
  childhood, 70–73
  of infants, 16, 23–5, 63–4, 67
  schizoid, 116
  sexual, 91–2
philosophers, 121–2
Plato, 76
pleasure principle, the, 11, 21
population control, 161–2
  animal, 53
population explosion, the, 53, 160–62
power:
  delusions of, 115–16
  will for, 10, 19, 37, 75

primitive man, 45, 57, 150–51, 161
  illnesses of, 112, 131–2
projection, 129
  paranoid, 129–30, 131–5
psycho-analysts, 16, 17, 80–81, 147, 148–9
psychopaths, aggressive, 137–46
psychotherapists, 12–13
punishment:
  of children, 127–8, 144–5
  legal, 143–4

Rapoport, Anatol, 152–3, 158
rejection, sexual, 98–9
religion, 80–81
resentment, 106
Rolfe, Frederick, 119–20
Romilly, Sir Samuel, 143
Russell, Bertrand, 77–8
Rycroft, Charles, 148–9

sadism, 18, 91, *see also* cruelty
Scandinavia, 146
scapegoats, 44, 132–3, 134
Schilder, Paul, 25
schizoid people, 115–22, 128–9, 131, 137
Schjelderup-Ebbe, T., 43
Schubert, Franz, 78
Scott, J. P., 31–2, 33, 36, 37
Segal, Hanna, 60
self-esteem, 97–9, 108–9
sexual instinct, the, 18–19, 33–4, 36, 37, 39
  deviations, 91–2
  female, 91
  male, 18, 91–2
  unrelated, 94
sexual relationships, the, 88–100

sexual selection, 42–3, 85–6
size of institutions, 155–6
snakes, 42–3, 104
societies:
  animal, 42–4, 57–8
  ideal, 17, 74–8
  ideological, 79–81
  pattern of, 45–6
  size of, 155–7
  under threat, 47–9
society, 51
Spitz, René A., 150
sport, 159
Stekel, Wilhelm, 81
Stern, Karl, 121
sublimation, 122
suicide, 10, 102, 103, 111, 112
Switzerland, 156
sympathy, excessive, 110–11

television, effects of, 62, 71–2
tension, 21, 37, 39
territoriality, 52–7
Thompson, Clara M., 65
threat, response to, 47–9

U.S.S.R., 156
under-developed countries, 157, 162
unmarried, the, 93–5

Utopias, 17, 74, 75–6, 78, 83, 154

violence, *see also* cruelty
  effect on children, 70–73, 87–8
  crimes of, 139
  psychopathic, 145–6
  as punishment, 143–5

war, 13
  behaviour in time of, 47–9
  freedom from, 77–8
  nuclear, 151–4
  ritualized, 58
Washburn, S. L., 44, 58, 128, 149
weapons:
  and distance, 151–3
  invention of, 151
  nuclear, 12, 13, 39, 78, 147, 151–4, 162–3
Wells, H. G., 77
West, D. J., 111
Western civilization, 112, 156, 161
Winnicott, D. W., 64, 70, 148
women, nature of, 88–9, 90, 117, *see also* female aggression *and* mothers
Wynne-Edwards, V. C., 51, 56, 159

FOR THE BEST IN PAPERBACKS, LOOK FOR THE 🐧

In every corner of the world, on every subject under the sun, Penguin represents quality and variety – the very best in publishing today.

For complete information about books available from Penguin – including Puffins, Penguin Classics and Arkana – and how to order them, write to us at the appropriate address below. Please note that for copyright reasons the selection of books varies from country to country.

In the United Kingdom: Please write to *Dept E.P., Penguin Books Ltd, Harmondsworth, Middlesex, UB7 0DA.*

If you have any difficulty in obtaining a title, please send your order with the correct money, plus ten per cent for postage and packaging, to *PO Box No 11, West Drayton, Middlesex*

In the United States: Please write to *Dept BA, Penguin, 299 Murray Hill Parkway, East Rutherford, New Jersey 07073*

In Canada: Please write to *Penguin Books Canada Ltd, 2801 John Street, Markham, Ontario L3R 1B4*

In Australia: Please write to the *Marketing Department, Penguin Books Australia Ltd, P.O. Box 257, Ringwood, Victoria 3134*

In New Zealand: Please write to the *Marketing Department, Penguin Books (NZ) Ltd, Private Bag, Takapuna, Auckland 9*

In India: Please write to *Penguin Overseas Ltd, 706 Eros Apartments, 56 Nehru Place, New Delhi, 110019*

In the Netherlands: Please write to *Penguin Books Netherlands B.V., Postbus 195, NL–1380AD Weesp*

In West Germany: Please write to *Penguin Books Ltd, Friedrichstrasse 10–12, D–6000 Frankfurt/Main 1*

In Spain: Please write to *Alhambra Longman S.A., Fernandez de la Hoz 9, E–28010 Madrid*

In Italy: Please write to *Penguin Italia s.r.l., Via Como 4, I-20096 Pioltello (Milano)*

In France: Please write to *Penguin Books Ltd, 39 Rue de Montmorency, F-75003 Paris*

In Japan: Please write to *Longman Penguin Japan Co Ltd, Yamaguchi Building, 2–12–9 Kanda Jimbocho, Chiyoda-Ku, Tokyo 101*

PENGUIN PSYCHOLOGY

Introduction to Jung's Psychology   Frieda Fordham

'She has delivered a fair and simple account of the main aspects of my psychological work. I am indebted to her for this admirable piece of work' – C. G. Jung in the Foreword

Child Care and the Growth of Love   John Bowlby

His classic 'summary of evidence of the effects upon children of lack of personal attention ... it presents to administrators, social workers, teachers and doctors a reminder of the significance of the family' – *The Times*

The Anatomy of Human Destructiveness   Erich Fromm

What makes men kill? How can we explain man's lust for cruelty and destruction? 'If any single book could bring mankind to its senses, this book might qualify for that miracle' – Lewis Mumford

Sanity, Madness and the Family   R. D. Laing and A. Esterson

Schizophrenia: fact or fiction? Certainly not fact, according to the authors of this controversial book. Suggesting that some forms of madness may be largely social creations, *Sanity, Madness and the Family* demands to be taken very seriously indeed.

The Social Psychology of Work   Michael Argyle

Both popular and scholarly, Michael Argyle's classic account of the social factors influencing our experience of work examines every area of working life – and throws constructive light on potential problems.

Check Your Own I.Q.   H. J. Eysenck

The sequel to his controversial bestseller, containing five new standard (omnibus) tests and three specifically designed tests for verbal, numerical and visual–spatial ability.

PENGUIN PSYCHOLOGY

Psychoanalysis and Feminism   Juliet Mitchell

'Juliet Mitchell has risked accusations of apostasy from her fellow feminists. Her book not only challenges orthodox feminism, however; it defies the conventions of social thought in the English-speaking countries ... a brave and important book' – *New York Review of Books*

Helping Troubled Children   Michael Rutter

Written by a leading practitioner and researcher in child psychiatry, a full and clear account of the many problems encountered by young school-age children – development, emotional disorders, underachievement – and how they can be given help.

The Divided Self   R. D. Laing

'A study that makes all other works I have read on schizophrenia seem fragmentary ... The author brings, through his vision and perception, that particular touch of genius which causes one to say "Yes, I have always known that, why have I never thought of it before?"' – *Journal of Analytical Psychology*

The Origins of Religion   Sigmund Freud

The thirteenth volume in the *Penguin Freud Library* contains Freud's views on the subject of religious belief – including *Totem and Taboo*, regarded by Freud as his best-written work.

The Informed Heart   Bruno Bettelheim

Bettelheim draws on his experience in concentration camps to illuminate the dangers inherent in all mass societies in this profound and moving masterpiece.

Introducing Social Psychology   Henri Tajfel and Colin Fraser (eds.)

From evolutionary changes to the social influence processes in a given group, a distinguished team of contributors demonstrate how our interaction with others and our views of the social world shape and modify much of what we do.